Women of Afghanistan in the Post-Taliban Era

Women of Afghanistan in the Post-Taliban Era

How Lives Have Changed and Where They Stand Today

ROSEMARIE SKAINE

McFarland & Company, Inc., Publishers
Jefferson, North Carolina, and London

Library of Congress Online Catalog Data

Skaine, Rosemarie.
    Women of Afghanistan in the post-Taliban era : how lives
have changed and where they stand today / Rosemarie Skaine.
      p.   cm.
    Includes bibliographical references and index.

    ISBN 978-0-7864-3792-4
    softcover : 50# alkaline paper ∞

    1. Women — Afghanistan.   2. Women — Legal status, laws,
etc. — Afghanistan.   3. Women — Religious aspects — Islam.
4. Women — Afghanistan — Social conditions. I. Title.
HQ1735.6.S385   2008
305.409581'090511 — dc22   2008034165
British Library cataloguing data are available

On the cover: For the first time in history, Afghan women pray
and read the Qur'an at a mosque in Kabul, October 17, 2004
(AFP Photo)

Manufactured in the United States of America

McFarland & Company, Inc., Publishers
  Box 611, Jefferson, North Carolina 28640
  www.mcfarlandpub.com

To Nasrine Abou-Bakre Gross,
who loves Afghanistan and
works to keep it free

Acknowledgments

Dr. Lina Abirafeh, gender and development professional, generously shared her research resulting from her study in Afghanistan between 2002 and 2006 on gendered interventions in the country. Her interviews with Afghan women and her photographs have significantly enriched this book.

Interviewees provided keen insights into the progress in Afghanistan: Nasrine Abou-Bakre Gross, founder of the Roqia Center for Women's Rights, Studies and Education in Afghanistan, an officially registered Afghan civil society organization that aims to assist the cause of women as an integral part of the country's democratization and reconstruction; the Honorable Haron Amin, ambassador, Embassy of the Islamic Republic of Afghanistan in Tokyo; the Honorable Dr. Zahir Tanin, ambassador, permanent representative of Afghanistan to the United Nations; and Professor Abdul Raheem Yaseer, assistant director of the Center for Afghanistan Studies, University of Nebraska at Omaha, United States.

Individuals who facilitated interviews were most helpful: Kathy Laubach, public affairs officer, Embassy of Afghanistan in Tokyo; May Mariano, assistant to Zahir Tanin; and staff members of the embassies of Afghanistan in Berlin and Sofia.

I am grateful to several people for assistance in finding photographs: Patricia Adams, USAID/LPA/SCP, a librarian at the United Nations, who helped me not only in acquiring photographs, but also generously assisted me in other ways; Jorge Jaramillo, senior account executive at Newscom in New York City; and Vladimir Bessarabov, cartographer, Department of Field Support, United Nations.

For his persevering assistance with the editing and proofreading of this, my eleventh book, I thank my best friend and husband, James C.

Skaine, professor emeritus in communication studies at the University of Northern Iowa.

Diane Brandt, my friend, provided timely news articles. Mary Nelson and Jane Teaford, also my friends, were supportive of my writing.

Robert Kramer, professor emeritus and founder of the Center for Social and Behavioral Research at UNI, advanced the book through his expertise in technology and statistics.

Richard L. Kuehner and Nancy L. Craft Kuehner and William V. Kuehner and Carolyn E. Guenther Kuehner provide ongoing support of my work.

I am forever grateful to Cass Paley, my friend of yesteryear, who came and gave without taking.

Table of Contents

List of Tables

Preface

The face of Afghanistan is changing. ... on a micro level of the women of Afghanistan, there are some very remarkable milestones that have been achieved.

— The Honorable Haron Amin, the ambassador at the embassy of the Islamic Republic of Afghanistan in Tokyo[1]

In the aftermath of 9/11, Afghanistan saw the overthrow of its oppressive Taliban rule. About this time my book *The Women of Afghanistan Under the Taliban* was published. I never imagined that it would be a part of the universal collective consciousness. Like many, I watched the unfolding events. My desire to learn and know more about the fate of the women of Afghanistan since 2001 led me to write this new book.

"When examining a complex issue such as women's roles in society, one must holistically consider the multiple factors at play,"[2] write Mitra K. Shavarini and Wendy R. Robison. Few, if any, considerations could be more important. Nasrine Abou-Bakre Gross, who has worked in education in Afghanistan since the Taliban were overthrown, writes about the culture of war in Afghanistan as does Dr. Sima Samar, who heads the Afghanistan Independent Human Rights Commission.

The context for women includes the destruction of war, poverty, corruption, geopolitical and regional power struggles, and familial, cultural and religious values.[3] Poverty and war lead to poor health, inaccessible schools and a lower quality of family and social life. This is the context in which Afghan people find themselves, and women, children and men are affected. But a lack of statistical data, as a result of a quarter of a century of war, makes it difficult to determine the extent to which women suffered, remarked Masooda Jalal, the Minister of Women's Affairs, in 2005.[4]

Haron Amin, the ambassador at the embassy of the Islamic Republic of Afghanistan in Tokyo, cautions, "Specific indicators or ... numbers in the context of women's employment or empowerment in Afghanistan are very, very difficult to find; as [are numbers related to] the problem of men's empowerment or lack thereof."[5]

I present indicators throughout this book, including social, demographic and conflict indicators, but I also ask the reader to interpret these statistics judiciously because they tell only part of the story. As Ambassador Amin says, "A lot of the projects are ongoing. We know that they will impact specific percentages or numbers of people and we also know that within those specific numbers or households there are also women.... What is significant is that, under the Taliban women were completely condemned to their houses, and ... this happens to be against the Afghan culture or tradition enduring for thousands of years.... Under the Taliban, women were condemned to their homes and had no active roles, but after the liberation of Afghanistan, these women are back at schools, they're back at their employment, they're back at the government offices. They're back at their businesses or they are back on their own farmland with their husbands. So, that means that actually there is a significant number of [women] employed in Afghanistan. It's just very difficult to determine it in the context of income, to express it in the context of numbers and census."[6]

Since many projects are in progress, Ambassador Amin says, "the face of Afghanistan is changing.... We believe that since the fall of the Taliban, Afghanistan's journey toward stability and development is in fact at full speed.... If we take a closer look, on a micro level [at] the women of Afghanistan, there are some very remarkable milestones that have been achieved."[7]

One remarkable challenge is that the country faces a positive problem, the problem of growth, for example, in education. More children are enrolled than current schools and teachers can handle. All of this progress is in the midst of conflict. Afghanistan, though, remains undaunted by the magnitude of rebuilding the infrastructure.

The women of Afghanistan are living within this context of challenge and growth. Although women face challenges, it is important to keep in mind that men do also. One of the areas undergoing social change is the change in the gender order. Dr. Lina Abirafeh writes, "While women may benefit from the increased emphasis placed on them by aid agencies, men tend to feel emasculated as a result. Failing to take Afghan gender dynamics into consideration increases social tensions."[8]

The aim of this book is to examine the status of women in Afghanistan in 2008 and to see how their lives are affected by the resurgence of the Taliban.

1

History and Background

Gender has ... been one of the most politicized issues in Afghanistan over the past 100 years.

— World Bank Report[1]

In Afghanistan, the link connecting the rights and role of Afghan women with the national destiny existed throughout the twentieth century. In 2006 the World Bank reported, "Women not only carry the burden of symbolizing the honor of the family, but often are seen as embodying the national honor as well."[2] Nasrine Abou-Gross who is helping to rebuild the Afghan education system, said in 2000, "If we write about Afghan women without understanding the political situation, we are going to hurt them even more."[3] Therefore, we must understand Afghan women within their history and their context.

Background

As the superpowers struggle with problems of nuclear weapons and terrorism, Louis Dupree's analysis in 1980 remains true today: Afghanistan, "created partly as a result of imperialism, but never a colony," may find achieving stability not impossible, but challenging.[4] The 1979 Soviet invasion of Afghanistan set off a reaction that linked Islamic jihadism to national liberation. The Afghans prevailed in their ten-year war when the Soviet Union departed in 1989.

The war was costly. The resistance rarely acknowledged its casualties, but approximately one million Afghan civilians were killed, and five

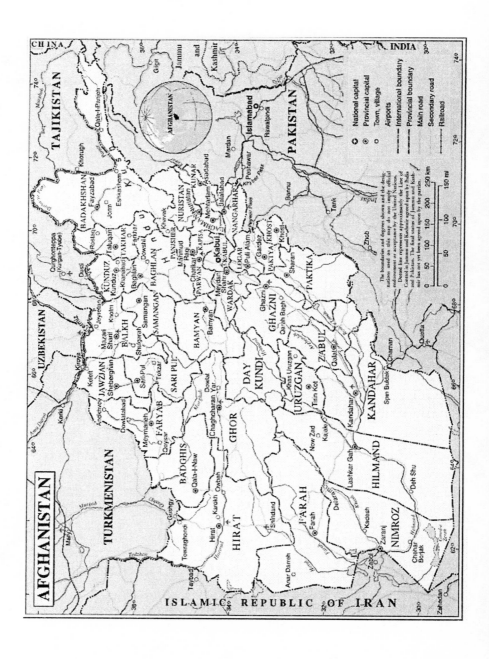

6

Table 1.1
The Afghan Population, 1999 and 2008

Age Group by Gender	1999 Number	Percent	2008 Number	Percent
Total	25,824,882	100.0	31,889,923	100.0
0–14 years	11, 063,301	42.8	14,222,978	44.6
male	5,640,841	22.8	7,282,600	22.8
female	5,422,460	21.0	6,940,378	21.8
15–64 years	14,050,431	54.4	16,895,557	53.0
male	7,273,681	28.2	8,668,170	27.2
female	6,776,750	26.2	8,227,387	25.8
65 years and over	711,150	2.8	711,388	2.4
male	374,666	1.5	374,426	1.2
female	336,484	1.3	396,962	1.2

Source: CIA, *World Fact Book*, "Afghanistan," January 1, 1999, and March 6, 2008, http://www.odci.gov/cia/publications/factbook/ and https://www.cia.gov/library/publications/the-world-factbook/geos/af.html (accessed January 30, 2000, and March 10, 2008).

million became refugees.[5] After the Soviet Union was defeated, Afghanistan was ravaged by civil war that continued even after the Mujahedeen government was formed in Kabul in 1992.

In 1994 the Taliban began capturing cities, with Kandahar being the first. In 1995 they gained control of Herat and in 1996, Jalalabad and Kabul. In 1998 a massacre took place in Mazar-I-Sharif, the same year that the United States fired missiles at alleged terrorist networks after the al-Qa'ida attacks on the United States Embassies in Kenya and Tanzania. As part of the Taliban's rise to power, they imposed severe restrictions on women.[6]

The Taliban's conservative views of holy scriptures led to stricter interpretations of what constituted socially acceptable female behavior. Women were subjected to grave violations of their human rights throughout the Taliban's reign. The Taliban regime justified its edicts saying that they were for the protection of women.[7] Taliban edicts and restrictions did not allow women free mobility and women were prohibited from employment, education or medical care. Women could not be examined by a

***Opposite*: United Nations map of Afghanistan, Map No. 3958 Rev. 5, October 2005. Department of Peacekeeping Operations, Cartographic Branch.**

male physician and only a few female doctors were allowed to work in the hospital in Kabul.[8]

Progress of the Afghan Government and of Women During Coalition War

In October 2001, coalition forces in response to terrorist actions of September 11, 2001, assisted in overthrowing the Taliban regime.[9] Afghan leaders met in Bonn, Germany, under the auspices of the special representative of the Secretary-General for Afghanistan to map out Afghanistan's future. The Bonn Agreement was signed on December 5, 2001. Members agreed on an interim power-sharing arrangement, the creation of a new constitution, and elections to be held in 2004. They put together a roadmap and timetable for establishing peace and security, reconstructing the country, reestablishing key institutions, and protecting human rights.[10] An interim government for two years took effect under the leadership of Hamid Karzai. The Bonn Agreement established an interim administration which included Dr. Sima Samar as vice-chair, Women's Affairs.[11] The Bonn agreement also specified that the Special Independent Commission of the interim government was to ensure that the representation in the Emergency Loya Jirga include a significant number of women. Afghanistan ratified its constitution on January 4, 2004, held a presidential election on October 9, 2004, and held parliamentary elections on September 18, 2005.[12]

After the 2004 election, the cabinet had three women ministers out of the twenty-seven appointed. Massouda Jalal, a medical doctor and President Karzai's only female opponent in the October 9 presidential election, was appointed minister of women's affairs. During her campaign for president, Jalal received death threats, the Associated Press reported. Sediqa Balkhi, who was appointed as the minister of martyrs and disabled, was one of three women who participated in the December 2001 Bonn Conference. She is a former teacher who has a bachelor's degree in Islamic Studies. Amina Afzali was appointed minister of youth affairs and also participated in the Bonn Conference. She also served on the Afghanistan Independent Human Rights Commission and the commission that drafted the new Afghan constitution.[13]

Other ministries created special programs dedicated to women, for

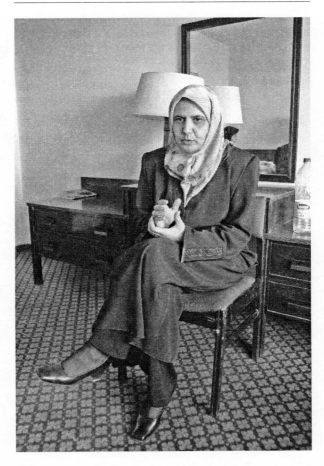

President of the Islamic Afghan Women's Movement Amina Afzali, 43, is dressed casually as she speaks to an AFP journalist at a hotel room in Kabul December 30, 2001. Amina, who fights for women's freedom in Afghanistan, says all Afghan women should take off their burqas as a symbol of liberation (AFP Photo/Jimin LAI).

example, the minister of foreign affairs created an Office of Human Rights, Health and Women's Affairs in the Ministry of Foreign Affairs. The Ministry of Commerce established a Department of Women's Entrepreneurship to help women establish their own businesses.[14]

Displacement of Population

Because of its strategic location between the Middle East, Central Asia and the Indian subcontinent, Afghanistan has long been fought over. After more than twenty years of civil war, continuing coalition–Taliban conflict, and the worst drought in thirty years, the country experienced widespread suffering and massive displacement of the population inside and outside its borders.[15] Flight to safety and displacement within is a familiar pattern for Afghanistan. One-third of the population fled the country during the Soviet occupation and the Taliban period. More than six million refugees sought refuge in Pakistan and Iran. Afghanistan was then the world's leading source of refugees, according to a UN report.[16]

After the fall of the Taliban in November 2001, refugees began returning to the country. With the help of the 2002 voluntary repatriation program with the office of the United Nations High Commissioner for Refugees (UNHCR), more than 3.5 million Afghans returned. Of this number, 2.7 million were from Pakistan and 800,000 from Iran. In 2007, the UNHCR estimated that 3.5 million refugees were still residing in Pakistan and Iran and that 150,000 internally displaced persons were in Afghanistan, mostly in the south.[17]

In 2008, more than two million illegal Afghan migrants live in Iran and Pakistan. The government of Pakistan is planning to close four Afghan refugee camps. This closing will result in about 150,000 Afghans returning to Afghanistan.[18]

In January 2007, 1,500 families were displaced in the southern province of Helmand due to armed conflict. About 15,000 families were displaced due to the fighting in the south in the latter part of 2006.[19]

In 2008, the number of refugees who had returned grew to about five million, with over four million under the UNHCR–assisted voluntary repatriation program.[20]

Resurgency of the Taliban

In 2005, the Taliban and other antigovernment forces intensified their insurgency in the predominantly Pashtun areas in southern Afghanistan. The year 2005 was deadly for coalition soldiers in Afghanistan and more than 1,500 Afghan civilians died.[21]

With these conditions, a Human Rights Watch report in late 2006 informed the world that Afghanistan was becoming a haven for human rights abusers, criminals and militant extremists. Many of these had in the past severely abused Afghans, especially women and girls. Their presence threatened Afghanistan's stability, as well as that of the region and the world.[22]

Resurgent Taliban forces, tribal militias, and rearmed warlords took advantage of the power vacuum in many parts of the country. They increasingly used bombings and assassinations that included attacks on "soft targets" such as schools, teachers and religious figures. Their goal: "to terrorize ordinary citizens and demonstrate the central government's inability to protect them."[23]

The NATO forces in the United Nations–mandated International Security Assistance Force extended their reach to include the entire country. The insurgency in southern and southeastern Afghanistan intensified into open warfare. Regional warlords and militias routinely subjected Afghans in other parts of the country to abuse. According to Human Rights Watch, most of them were ostensibly allied with the government. This alliance resulted in "poor governance and corruption of the government of President Hamid Karzai, which often lacked the will or the capacity to protect the rights of ordinary Afghans."[24] Afghans were disappointed and frustrated by the lack of coordinated international security and financial assistance.

In 2006, the Taliban proved to be more brutal and deadly than the forces the United States threw out in 2001. The Taliban became a new terror and turned Afghanistan into the most dangerous place in the world, according to *National Geographic*. The Taliban resurfaced intensely, using roadside bombings, direct fire and suicide attacks.[25]

In September 2006, in a hearing of the U.S. House of Representatives Committee on International Relations, the committee declared Afghanistan to be on the brink of becoming a failed state. Retrained Taliban were showing their strength in new attacks that appeared to be influenced by the spiraling Iraqi insurgency. The committee believed, "Reinforcing the democratic successes in Afghanistan is critical to supporting its national reconciliation process and rebuilding a viable and independent nation-state that is secure and free from terrorism."[26] Chair Henry Hyde stressed that only through a comprehensive approach of fighting terrorism and corruption, would the United States quicken reconstruction on the ground, improve the quality of life for Afghan citizens and help win the war against the Taliban. The U.S. commanding officer in Afghanistan, General Karl Eikenberry, emphasized the link between reconstruction and violence: "Wherever the roads end, that is where the Taliban starts."[27] In a letter to the president of the United States, Chairman Hyde outlined the additional problem of the increase of almost 60 percent in illicit opium production in 2006 which strengthened warlord support of anti-coalition forces such as the Taliban. Hyde believed the efforts of the United States were failing and that Afghanistan faced its highest levels of violence and corruption since its liberation. Hyde believed that the United States should move away from its eradication program to focus on drug kingpins, their warlord allies, heroin production labs and trade routes.[28]

In December 2007, NATO and the United States remained very concerned about the possibility that they would fail in Afghanistan. Reviewing their mission in the country, they acknowledged the need for greater coordination in fighting the Taliban and al-Qa'ida, stopping the rising opium production and trafficking that finances the insurgency, and assisting the Kabul government to expand its legitimacy and control. The routing of Taliban and al-Qa'ida forces after the attacks of September 11, 2001, is one of the United States administration's most important legacies, but it may slip away.[29]

The NATO alliance is committed to getting people to look beyond 2008 and understand the conflict as a longer-term effort. The U.S. administration has a sense that the 2007 troop buildup in Iraq turned around a dangerous situation, but that the effort in Afghanistan has begun to drift, at best.[30]

The Democratic chairman of the House Armed Services Committee, Representative Ike Skelton of Missouri, assessed possible failure in Afghanistan, saying, "I have a real concern that given our preoccupation in Iraq, we've not devoted sufficient troops and funding to Afghanistan to ensure success in that mission.... Afghanistan has been the forgotten war." But resources are strained due to U.S. commitments in Iraq. Admiral Mike Mullen, chairman of the Joint Chiefs of Staff, told Congress, "In Afghanistan, we do what we can. In Iraq, we do what we must."[31]

In 2007, Transparency International, the Global Coalition Against Corruption, ranked Afghanistan 172 out of 179 countries in their Corruptions Perceptions Index, scoring 1.8 out of a possible 10. "CPI Score relates to perceptions of the degree of corruption as seen by business people and country analysts, and ranges between 10 (highly clean) and 0 (highly corrupt)."[32] Denmark ranked first making it the most clean, scoring 9.4 and Somalia placed last making it the most corrupt, 179, scoring 1.4.

Afghanistan, Iraq, Myanmar, Sudan and Somalia remain at the bottom of the index. Transparency International explains that a low score does not imply the people are corrupt for they are often the victims of corruption. In addition, they write, "Countries torn apart by conflict pay a huge toll in their capacity to govern. With public institutions crippled or nonexistent, mercenary individuals help themselves to public resources and corruption thrives."[33] Previously, in 2005, Transparency International evaluated Afghanistan and ranked it 117 out of 158 countries giving it a score of 2.5.[34]

While these problems are real, other problems deserve focus as well, according to Dr. Barnett Rubin, renowned expert on Afghanistan. From interviews on his twenty-sixth trip to Afghanistan Rubin found,

> a universal belief in the region and in Afghanistan that success in Afghanistan is not a high priority for the United States, and people cite in this the amount of our funding, the level of our troop presence, the invasion of Iraq, and many other things that we have been doing. When people in the region believe that success in Afghanistan is not a high priority for the United States, they make arrangements to protect their interests in the absence of the United States. Therefore, they keep their clients on the ready, and they prepare to fill what they believe will be a power vacuum. And in a way, that is the fundamental cause of the things that are going wrong in Afghanistan.[35]

> The insurgency is undermining that security. You cannot defeat an insurgency that has a safe haven. The center of global terrorism today is in Pakistan. It is not in Iraq. It is not in Lebanon. It is in Pakistan. That is why Pakistan cooperates with us so much, because al-Qaeda is in Pakistan, and the Taliban are also in Pakistan.[36]

Ambassador Haron Amin lends support to Rubin's views:

> On the regional level, we have to be very cautious and very clear that all sanctuaries in the region, all sanctuaries that make up the greater

terrorist infrastructure must be uprooted. In this context, we believe that regional dialogues and get-togethers will help peoples in the enlightened segments of society to get together, to engage in specific activities to be able to lessen or reduce the role that Taliban or like-minded individuals make.[37]

On an international level, I want to highlight two points. One, we believe that the international consensus on the war on terror is lacking the drive to muster up sufficient troops, equipment and support to close the regional resurgence of Taliban and al-Qa'ida. And second, the international consensus in the campaign to turn Afghanistan into a functioning democracy with a sustaining economy has lacked the will to pledge ... on a per capita basis the same amount as in other regions' post-conflict countries. I mean Rwanda; I mean Bosnia; I mean Kosovo. There needs to be more pledging of assistance to Afghanistan.[38]

Professor Abdul Raheem Yaseer, assistant director of the Center for Afghanistan Studies at the University of Nebraska at Omaha, believes that the situation in Afghanistan "generally is not very good because the purpose that the United States and the international community have been trying to achieve has been a failure." He gives the following reasons for the lack of success:

It has been a failure in the area of maintaining security which was the main objective. The other objective was to eliminate terrorists. That has not been achieved because the terrorists and Taliban are back. Security has not been maintained. There is terrorist infiltration from the borders; suicide bombers and Taliban and Pakistanis. Many come with arms and kill Americans and international forces and Afghan national army [personnel]. The drug [trafficking] was supposed to be eliminated ... drug cultivation, drug processing. That has failed. So none of these three goals has been achieved, but other things have been achieved, for example, in education and for women.[39]

Almost all people in the United States believe that the initial response of the United States to 9/11, that of aligning with Afghanistan, was good. Unfortunately, the United States got side-tracked when it went to war in Iraq, and Afghanistan suffered from our scattered focus.

In 2008, the Center for the Study of the Presidency in the United States recommended in part "decoupling Iraq and Afghanistan in the U.S. legislative process and in the management of these conflicts in the Executive branch."[40] The bipartisan group asserted, the United States and the international community have tried to win the struggle in Afghanistan with too few military forces, insufficient economic aid, and without a clear and consistent comprehensive strategy to fill the power vacuum outside Kabul and counter the combined challenges of reconstituted Taliban and al-Qaeda forces in Afghanistan and Pakistan, a runaway opium economy, and the stark poverty faced by most Afghans.[41]

Further, the study reported that accomplishing success in Afghanistan will require a sustained, multi-year commitment to make the war in Afghanistan and its reconstruction a higher U.S. foreign policy priority. Although substantial obstacles remain, failure in Afghanistan would bring severe consequences for long-term U.S. interests in the region and for security at home. The report maintains that the United States must revitalize its efforts and rethink strategies so that Afghanistan can be stabilized. The U.S. commitment level should be commensurate with the threat posed by possible failure in Afghanistan.[42]

Increase in Insurgency Attacks

In April 2007, Amnesty International reported that Taliban attacks against Afghan civilians were increasing and taking the form of suicide attacks, abductions and beheadings. At least 756 civilians were killed in 2006 in attacks that used improvised explosive devices such as roadside bombs and in suicide attacks, according to UN and NATO figures.[43]

The attacks were used to instill fear and exercise control. The attacks targeted teachers, aid workers, school buildings, women's rights activists, clerics, government workers and health workers. The Taliban's widespread indiscriminate killing and the killing of civilians are war crimes and crimes against humanity. According to Amnesty International, the Taliban's response is that "there is no difference between the armed people who are fighting against us and civilians who are co-operating with foreigners."[44]

Twice as many Afghans (3,000) died from violence in 2006 as in 2005, more than in any other year since the 2001 fall of the Taliban. The United Nations estimated that the violence in southern Afghanistan displaced 15,000 families or approximately 80,000 people.[45]

In November 2007, Taliban attacks continued to rise. The number

15

of improvised explosive devices (IEDs), including car and suicide bombs, totaled 1,932, up from 1,739 for all of 2006 and up from 782 in 2005. The year 2007 was the bloodiest in Afghanistan since the fall of the Taliban.[46] Barnett Rubin, an Afghanistan expert at New York University, says that greater use of bombs shows the Taliban are gaining momentum. They do not launch conventional attacks. "They've gone back to guerilla warfare ... because it works."[47]

On February 21, 2008, *Guardian Unlimited* states that despite the presence of NATO troops and billions of dollars in aid, "The Taliban has a permanent presence in 54 percent of Afghanistan and the country is in serious danger of falling into the group's hands."[48] The Senlis Council, an independent thinktank, released a report stating that the insurgency is also exercising a "significant amount of psychological control, gaining more and more political legitimacy in the minds of the Afghan people, who have a long history of shifting alliances and regime change."[49] In addition, the Council echoes a UN and Oxfam warning that the frontline is getting ever closer to Kabul and more and more of the country is becoming a "no go" area for western aid and development workers. The situation is grave. The United States and Britain need to increase their troops and countries not involved, for example, France and Germany, need to become committed.

Finally, in November 2007, the U.S. administration assessed the war, concluding that "wide-ranging strategic goals that the Bush administration set for 2007 have not been met, even as U.S. and NATO forces have scored significant combat successes against resurgent Taliban fighters."[50]

In January 2008, Dr. Larry Goodson, Afghanistan specialist at the U.S. Army War College, underscored that the Taliban has returned as a serious threat and that the year 2007 proved to be the bloodiest year since they were ousted in 2001. The Afghanistan NGO Safety Office stated that the Taliban's departure in 2001 was more of a strategic retreat than an actual military defeat.[51] Further the office said that 2008 cannot be expected to be any better than 2007[52]; it states, "In simple terms, the consensus among informed individuals at the end of 2007 seems to be that Afghanistan is at the beginning of a war, not the end of one."[53]

Graeme Smith writes, "One [Vigilant Strategic Services Afghanistan] analysis shows violence in the country has already increased 15 percent, compared with the beginning of last year."[54] The 15 percent increase represents 389 violent attacks. Some western observers have begun referring to the rise in bloodshed as the beginning of a bigger war. Two Kabul security consultancies suggest a slightly less dismal view, reporting Taliban attacks falling somewhat in the final months of 2007.

The early trend for the year suggests the Taliban may have refocused their efforts on the south, including Kandahar. The southern region represented 41 percent of insurgent attacks in the first three weeks, compared with 25 percent in 2007.[55] Except for refusing to send soldiers into the dangerous south, NATO gives a conflicting report. The Taliban insurgency is not spreading, in spite of recent pessimistic reports, NATO says. The organization reports that three-fourths of Afghanistan suffered one violent incident per week, and that 70 percent of the violence in 2007 occurred in just 10 percent of the country.[56]

Ambassador Haron Amin evaluates the reasons for the resurgence of the Taliban locally, nationally, regionally and internationally. Locally, he gives the following reasons:

> Although the Afghan security forces have been able to take on the Taliban, they were not sufficient, they were not enough to combat the Taliban. Weak judiciary so far has led to the mullahs acting as judges. People have had their disputes. They wanted to resolve them, could not find appropriate judges or courts, so they went to the local mullah to get a verdict or a decree. Another weakness: weak and at times corrupt government institutions have disillusioned the populace about the future. Poverty and underdevelopment proved the Taliban claim that life is not changing. The fact is [that] a huge number of people lived in underdevelopment, mostly living under a dollar a day, although that is actually changing. That is changing because people today live better; they're happier.... Incredibly, every day of the week that I was there some wedding was happening. Kabul is just booming with all of these restaurants and ... wedding salons.[57]

Poverty has a trickling effect all over Afghanistan, explains Amin. It is not limited to rural areas or to urban areas. He explains the misperceptions, "A lot of people say that the rural people know that Kabul city is doing better, and so a lot of people from the rural areas are moving to Kabul to seek jobs, and, as a result, jobs are not found and people do not have as much money as before. Then ... they move back to the countryside and they become even poorer. Overall, however, I think that what we see is progress and living better across Afghanistan."[58]

Regionally, the infiltration of Taliban from Pakistan has not been successfully addressed, and nationally, says Amin:

> The war on terror was labeled an easy victory and sidetracked by other issues. We don't really believe that enough resources were provided to combat the Taliban. On a per capita basis, Afghanistan has received less money compared to other post-conflict countries. Also, precision bombing or targeting [by the coalition forces] led to civilian casualties. And unfortunately, labeled by a lot of the international forces as collateral damage [thus] the Taliban label or paint the war as a crusade against Muslims.[59]

Afghan Women in Context of Results of 2001–08

In 2006, the United Nations Development Fund for Women reported that even though there was room for improvement, women were increasingly visible in all sectors of society: commerce, communications, technology, engineering, media, public works, mines, industry, security, defense and education.[60]

In 2007, Ileana Ros-Lehtinen (R–Florida), member of the U.S. House of Representatives Committee on Foreign Affairs, said that the highlight of the progress in Afghanistan since the removal of the Taliban was the advances of women. The people enjoy new freedoms. Women are taking part in political and economic life. Schools and clinics are being built. Economic development is in progress. As militant extremists seek to reclaim Afghanistan as a safe haven for their activities, the security situation threatens the progress. Ros-Lehtinen reported that the drug trade is a primary factor contributing to the resurgency of the Taliban because the proceeds allow them to finance sophisticated weapons used to target citizens of Afghanistan and coalition forces.[61]

In 2007, Professor Yaseer shared insights into the causes of the resurgence of the Taliban and its relationship to progress for women in society as well as for society as a whole:

> As you know, the Taliban were supposed to be totally eliminated. They were not eliminated. They were just pushed out of Afghanistan into

Pakistan where they found safe havens with the support of the Pakistan military. They had camps and schools and madrasas where they got more training. Their training did not stop, it continued. They received more money and arms and facilities. Therefore, they were not totally eliminated. As a matter of fact, they were supported. Then when the attention was diverted from Afghanistan to Iraq, that provided a good opportunity for the Taliban who went into Pakistan to get reunited. Their supporters, Saudi Arabia being part of [this group and the] Pakistani military [being another] part of it, and some other elements here and there, helped them to get reorganized, to regroup and then they were allowed to infiltrate into Afghanistan and kill teachers, warn women and burn schools. They caused insecurity and issued threats. Even now, in Kabul, when you go there, you see hundreds and thousands of teachers, who are going to school, still wearing the burqa because they fear the infiltration of the Taliban from abroad. The Afghans themselves, no matter how conservative they are, they love their children, sons and daughters, to get an education. They would never do things that would jeopardize this lofty goal. But, the outsiders, the Taliban and, to some extent, the Pakistan government, are not in favor of educating and doing good in Afghanistan. They want to keep the women deprived of their rights, of their right to education, and keep them ignorant. These are the major causes of not more progress being made in this area.[62]

The *Afghanistan Human Development Report 2007* indicated that, in spite of decades of war and suffering, Afghanistan continues to make progress in achieving its development goals. The *Report* says, "The GDP [Gross Domestic Product] per capita (in purchasing power parity terms) has increased from U.S. $683 in 2002 to U.S. $964 in 2005. An additional 132,000 square kilometers of land was cleared of landmines in 2006. The number of telephone users shot up to 2.5 million (or 10 percent of the population). School enrollment has grown in the past five years from approximately 900,000 to nearly 5.4 million, and the prevalence of malaria and tuberculosis has dropped dramatically."[63]

The NATO indicators reflect even more dramatic improvements (see Table 1.2 on following page). The International Security Assistance Force mission is to bring lasting peace and stability back to the country so that speedy reconstruction and development can take place. The Force activities include identification of needs such as the rehabilitation of schools and medical facilities, the restoration of water supplies, and the provision

Table 1.2
Reconstruction and Development Achievements in Numbers, June 2007

Reconstruction and Development Achievements in Numbers:

- In 2001, 8% of Afghans had access to basic healthcare. In early 2007, the figure was up to 83%.
- In 2001, 1.2 million children attended school daily; by June 2007, 7 million do, including 2 million girls. A total of 43,000–45,000 teachers were trained in 2006.
- 82 percent of the ring road network is open to traffic, through portions are still under construction.
- There were 88,136 anti-personnel mines destroyed, as well as 11,524 anti-tank mines.

Health:

- 83% of the population have access to medical facilities, compared to 9 percent in 2004
- 76% of children under the age of five have been immunized against childhood diseases
- More than 4,000 medical facilities opened since 2004
- Over 600 midwives were trained and deployed in every province of Afghanistan

Economy:

- GDP growth estimates of between 12–14% for the current year
- Government revenues increased by around 25% from 2005–06 to 2006–07
- Income per capita of $355, compared to $180 three years prior
- Afghanistan is one of the fastest growing economies in Southeast Asia

Private Sector:

- 10% of Afghans now own a mobile phone, compared to 2 per 1000 people in 2001
- 150 cities across Afghanistan now have access to mobile phone networks and Internet provider services
- Multinationals and internationals operating or showing an interest in Afghanistan include Coca-Cola, Siemens, Nestle and Etisalat
- Evidence of strong consumer demand in Kabul (e.g., road traffic, new shopping malls, new hotels)

Infrastructure:

- Over 4000 km of roads completed
- Work has begun on 20,000 new homes for Afghans returning to Kabul
- Over 1 billion square meters of mine contaminated land cleared
- 17,000 communities benefited from development programs such as wells, schools, hospitals and roads through the Government's National Solidarity Program

Security:
- Over 60,000 excombatants disarmed and reintegrated
- 35–40,000 officers are serving in the new national police force
- 30,000 soldiers are serving in the new national army

Refugees:
- 4.8 million have returned so far (3.5 million with the UN's help)
- The UN refugee agency has helped provide over 1 million shelters for returning refugees

Women:
- Over a quarter of parliamentarians are women
- Millions of girls are back in school, with 400,000 new female students starting school for the first time
- Over 100,000 women benefited from microfinance loans to set up businesses

Schools:
- Over 7 million girls and boys are in school or higher education
- 10 universities around the country, up from one (barely functioning) under the Taliban

Media:
- 7 national TV stations (6 private); numerous radio networks, plus a diverse and increasingly robust and professional print media

Source: "NATO in Afghanistan: Reconstruction and Development (June 2007 and November 15, 2007)," NATO, http://www/nato.int/issues/Afghanistan/factsheets/reconst_develop.html (accessed August 10, 2008) and http://www.nato.int/ISAF/topics/recon_dev/index.html (accessed December 26, 2007).

of appropriate support for other civil-military projects. In addition, indicators provided by the U.S. Agency for International Development (USAID) reflect that, in spite of the challenging conditions, Afghanistan has succeeded, with international help, in ten major areas. In fact, USAID refers to the period of time after twenty-two years of war and Taliban repression as Afghanistan's "rebirth."[64]

Further, the *Human Development Report* indicates that although Afghanistan's Human Development Index (HDI) has a value of 0.345, ranking far behind its neighbors at 174 out of 178 countries globally, factors exist that explain why this is so. These factors include hunger (6.6 million Afghans do not meet their minimum food requirements), gender discrimination, and, in 2006, a significant rise in terrorist attacks and a 59 percent increase in poppy cultivation, making the country the world leader in the production of illegal opium, accounting for 90 percent of

Table 1.3
Ten Major Achievements of Afghanistan, January 2007

1. Democratic elections: 7 million voted for president in 2004, and for parliament and provincial councils in 2005.
2. Roads link the country: Kabul-Kandahar road built; Kandahar-Herat road nearly complete; 800 km of local roads.
3. Agricultural output rises: Grain up 24%; livestock and poultry income up $200 million.
4. Fighters choose peace: 60,000 ex-combatants gave up weapons and joined civilian work force.
5. Domestic revenue up: $260 million in 2005.
6. Healthcare expands: 7 million people now reached.
7. Older students catch up: 170,000 make up lost years in accelerated learning program.
8. Construction expands: Thousands of homes and offices are built in cities and towns.
9. Five million refugees return: Largest return in history continues from Pakistan refugee camps and Iran.
10. Education booms: 3.2 million boys and 1.8 million girls enrolled.

Source: Afghanistan Now, January 2007, USAID, http://www.usaid.gov/locations/asia_near_east/countries/afghanistan/pdsf/afgh_now_0107.pdf (accessed January 2, 2008).

global production.[65] To improve the HDI, the Human Poverty Index (HPI) must be calculated. Afghanistan's HPI is one of the worst in the world with a more than 40 percent probability at birth of not surviving to age 40. Other HPI factors include adult literacy (76.5 percent in Afghanistan), population lacking access to clean water (68 percent), and children under five who are underweight (50 percent).[66] The Gender Development Index (GDI) is also considered in the HDI; it includes the same factors, but breaks them down according to gender. The GDI for women stands at .310, reflecting the inequality in opportunity faced by women in Afghanistan.[67] Although overall Afghanistan has progressed in its GDI with a slight increase since the *National Human Development Report 2004*, it still ranks below all other countries except Niger (292).

Economic growth is occurring rapidly, according to Amin. From 2002 to 2006, each year's growth has been 11 percent and in 2007 it was 13–17 percent. And that means, says Amin, that

> regionally, it is being pushed to produce; locally, it's being pushed to produce; nationally, it's being pushed to produce. For example, there

is a new initiative from the Ministry of Rural Development that, in the next ten years, a project will be the empowerment of rural areas. It is derived from the concept of the Japanese "One village, one product." So, each village or each province determines [which] one or two products that they make best, [and] that product is going to be marketed not only for local consumption, but national consumption and beyond for regional and international consumption. It has been determined that the project will take ten years and it will cost a couple billion dollars, but in the end it's going to employ 1.2 million people. The great majority of those are going to be women.[68]

The World Bank predicts that in 2008 the Gross Domestic Product growth rate could reach 13 percent. Afghanistan's foreign direct investment has been enjoying double-digit growth since 2002. M. Ashraf Haidari, political counselor at the Afghanistan embassy in Washington, D.C., writes, "A key aspect to Afghanistan's democratization, and the eventual defeat of radical Islamic militants, is maintaining the growth pace."[69]

Progress Continues and Challenges Remain for Women

In spite of the progress in the country, Afghan women and girls continue to suffer extremely low social, economic, and political status. The Human Rights Watch reported that indicators rank them among the world's least well off.[70] The *Afghanistan Human Development Report 2007* indicates that the existing enormous gender gap must be narrowed to meet goal three of the country's Millennium Development Goals, "Promote gender equality and empower women." This gap is manifested in the literacy rate, limited economic opportunities, discrimination and violence. On the plus side, women represent 25 percent of the National Assembly. Progress is occurring toward meeting the fourth development goal, to reduce child mortality. The infant mortality rate has decreased from $^{165}/_{1000}$ to $^{135}/_{1000}$—resulting in 40,000 additional successful births per year. Factors that contribute to the still relatively high child mortality rate include low literacy, unsafe drinking water, hunger, and poor sanitation. The fifth goal, to improve maternal health, stems from the fact that Afghanistan has one of the highest maternal mortality rates in the world, with the ratio estimated at 1,600 deaths per 100,000 live births.[71]

Women's social existence in some parts of the country needs improvement, according to the Human Rights Watch 2007 report. That many women and girls still cannot travel without an accompanying male relative and without wearing a burqa are examples that barriers still exist for them to work outside the home or move freely about society on their own.[72]

To fully understand the restrictions that remain in place on women in Afghanistan, it is critical to understand the larger context, society. The Revolutionary Association of Women of Afghanistan (RAWA) advocates a democratic and secular government as the only way to help Afghan people and particularly women. RAWA member Zoya said, "No doubt the war on terror toppled the misogynist and barbaric regime of Taliban. But it did not remove Islamic fundamentalism, which is the root cause of misery for all Afghan people; it just replaced one fundamentalist regime with another."[73] Another member of RAWA, Mariam Rawi, describes Afghanistan in 2006 this way,

> You might expect me to talk about Afghanistan as a free, peaceful and liberated country but painfully and unfortunately the reality is not what you might be aware of through media. After September 11, and the subsequent U.S. military intervention in Afghanistan in the name of "war on terror" and "liberating Afghan women," despite tall claims of [the] USA and its allies, Afghanistan is still burning in twofold fire. On the one hand, there are the brutal and horrific Jihadi fundamentalists of the "Northern Alliance" who are supported by the USA and on the other hand, there are the Taliban and al-Qa'ida terrorists who have the support of all the fundamentalist and terrorist regimes, parties and organizations in different parts of world.[74]

In 2005, Amnesty International reported that violence against women and girls is pervasive and few escape the reality or threat of violence. The forms of violence include abduction and rape by armed individuals, forced marriage, being traded by men settling disputes and debts, and discrimination in all segments of society. Strict societal codes, invoked in the name of tradition and religion, justify denying women fundamental rights and have led to the imprisonment and even the killing of some women.[75]

Violence by husbands and brothers is reinforced by authorities and tolerated by communities. Rights of women are difficult to obtain in a country with nearly thirty years of instability, but according to Amnesty International the need to combat violence against women is gaining ground. Although mainly in urban areas, women are coming forward to complain or to assert their rights. In both urban and rural areas, female networks of human rights defenders are forming.[76]

In "Lifting the Veil," a documentary on television's CNN, Sharmeen Obaid-Chinoy, a Muslim journalist, returned to Afghanistan to see whether things had changed since the Taliban had been overthrown. She found that troublesome issues existed, but that there were some "pockets of hope."[77] Among the bothersome findings: women beggars in Kabul, self-immolation, the selling of girls into marriage, increased risk for educated women and female activists such as RAWA members, resistance at home for women's advancement (including education and medical care), lack of schools and funds for education, poverty, and danger on the front lines of war.[78]

Although progress is slow, hope appeared in places least expected, said Obaid-Chinoy. Traveling to western Afghanistan, she found "new roads and power, six times the number of students in school, even a feeling of peace in some places, like Herat."[79] In the small town of Talakan in the northeast of Afghanistan, she reported that the rebuilding taking place was in contrast to some of the most intense fighting between the allies and the Taliban in 2001. In Talakan she noted the sounds of laughter and play of young schoolgirls on the playground and within the school. In northern Afghanistan in Takitanuz, where the Taliban had had a base just outside the town, young boys and girls now study together in the school. But not all problems have been solved by the invasion. Aid has not always come or reached people most in need.

Ambassador Haron Amin reminds us that neither gender lives in isolation:

> What we need to do is basically to make every single member of the Afghan society, be it woman or man, [a part of] the active agenda of development in the country. I believe as such, we can take Afghanistan and put it in the twenty-first century. I hope that you understand that on the agenda of the Afghan government, women, in fact, are more important than men. That is the advocacy of President Karzai, that is my advocacy and that of the new generation of Afghans. We strongly

believe that, for as long as we have segments of society deprived of their fundamental rights, we will not attain development in the true sense.[80]

Dr. Lina Abirafeh's study also emphasizes the principle that neither gender lives in isolation. Her research for a Ph.D. dissertation was done between 2002 and 2006 on gendered interventions in Afghanistan. She found that "a prominent aid intervention with a high-profile focus on gender ... demonstrates that gender initiatives that lack men's engagement will likely not achieve gender equality and will fail to achieve the ultimate goals of poverty alleviation and sustainable development."[81]

It is important to note the human rights treaties Afghanistan has ratified. Among these are the International Convention on the Elimination of all forms of Discrimination against Women, the International Covenant on Civil and Political Rights and the UN Convention on the Rights of the Child.[82]

Pakistan Connection

Pakistan's role in the development of the Taliban was critical and, through continued tolerance, the country continues to provide much of the strength and support for the Taliban in its border regions.[83] Professor Yaseer believes that one of the complicating factors has been the U.S. support of Pakistan because the United States believes that Pakistan has been supportive in its "war on terror." He states,

> The problem is [that] the policy is not very clear, despite the fact that, from the soldiers to the generals to the presidents, they all know that the problem of war and the killing, the suicide bombing in Afghanistan ... have their core offense in Pakistan, but they have been turning a deaf ear and blind eye to the situation. I don't know what the policy is. They have not been doing anything to stop the problem at its source. Of course, they reinforced the camps and military installations inside Afghanistan with concrete buildings and concrete walls and blocks, barbed wire and binoculars and spy glasses and reconnaissance flights, but they haven't done anything to eliminate the sources and they haven't stopped people from crossing the border. They come in, and they go around the camps and fortified installations, and they wait, and as soon as a convoy or a vehicle leaves with some personnel, then they bump

into them and explode themselves among the innocent people and the soldiers and vehicles. Everybody from all the fifty some countries represented in Afghanistan knows that the core of the problem is in Pakistan, for suicide bombings, for interferences, for drug trading, but they still keep pouring more and more dollars, billions of dollars, into Pakistan. They waive their loans. So they receive more financial aid than Afghanistan. Still they are asking for more. They are asking for payment for the air spaces that we use, for air bases that American forces and other nations' forces use. They get a lot of money. They lie about the al-Qa'ida members because they receive one million dollars for each head and they surrender innocent people or people with no immigration documents and call them terrorists. Most of the al-Qa'ida people that have been caught have been caught by American forces or by Afghans, not by Pakistanis, but they were caught in the territory of Pakistan so the Pakistanis want to get the credit for it.[84]

Yaseer believes that the Pakistan situation is a sad story and

has a very direct effect on the state of a woman in Afghanistan because these terrorists, these Taliban, are all extremist elements. They have an extremist approach toward treating women and they are not for women's liberation at all and they are not even for women to have education. They are just too fanatic about this. This causes a lot of problems. They have schools and universities for their women in Pakistan, in Saudi Arabia, in Lebanon. You see them on TV shows. They have all got their things, but as soon as a woman walks out on the street with high-heeled shoes or with no burqa, they raise hell. They have all kinds of modern entertainment involving their women on TV shows, pornography, films and movies, they are all shown in Afghanistan. It might be by satellite dishes, while the Afghan women are oppressed so much by these elements.[85]

This ill-treatment of women is not in effect as much as it was when I wrote *Women of Afghanistan Under the Taliban* in 2001. The Taliban's formal decrees are no more, but their edicts are still informally in effect, with the resurgence of the Taliban causing women to be fearful. Yaseer says that Afghan women are very brave. For example, he says, "When you go to Kabul and all over Afghanistan and you see the kinds of things the terrorists do, the explosions, the harassment, you think that they should not leave their homes, but they do. They go to school, they go to the ministry, they go to the provinces, they join the NGOs, they work in the foreign offices, they work with non–Islamic organizations. They are very brave. Unfortunately there is not much support for them and there is not much effort in eliminating these threats for them."[86]

In 2007, Amnesty International reported that Pakistan was continuing to support local and Afghan Taliban. The fighters had reportedly regrouped, resupplied, and directed attacks from bases in the western border regions in Pakistan, notably the Northwest Frontier Province, the Federally Administrated Tribal Areas, and parts of Baluchistan. Little interference from the Pakistani authorities was apparent.[87] But in 2008 the Pakistani military launched a series of strikes against a pro–Taliban stronghold in a tribal region on its border with Afghanistan. One of the key targets was a Taliban leader who the Pakistani government maintained orchestrated the December 27, 2007, assassination of opposition leader Benazir Bhutto.[88]

In mid–December 2007, the Taliban in Pakistan united as the Taliban Movement of Pakistan. Estimates of their fighting force number up to 40,000. The group chose as its leader Baitullah Mehsud, the man Pakistan accuses of murdering former prime minister Benazir Bhutto. The Taliban in Afghanistan and Pakistan share ideological goals but have separate structures. One-eyed mullah Mohammed Omar is the spiritual head of both and was the leader of the Afghan Taliban before they were ousted in 2001.[89]

Complicating this activity and in the face of evidence to the contrary is President Musharraf's denial of support of the Taliban, reports Amnesty International. In addition, Afghan government officials have urged Pakistani authorities to stop Taliban infiltration while U.S. officials praise Pakistan as a "key ally" in the "war on terror." Pakistani officials reject criticism, saying that Pakistan would take steps on any "actionable material as to where Taliban leaders are," provided by the U.S. or NATO forces.[90]

The United States Institute for Peace reported that Afghanistan and Pakistan have had largely antagonistic relations under all governments but the Taliban since Pakistan was created as part of the partition of India in 1947. In 2006 the Taliban and al-Qa'ida insurgencies were equally active in Afghanistan and Pakistan. Pakistani leaders maintained that the nationalist insurgency in Pakistani Baluchistan received support from Indian agents in Afghanistan. This assertion exacerbated relations between the two countries. Formation of a border area policy is essential to the vital interests of the United States, NATO and the international community. The Institute report says that Afghanistan, Pakistan and India must agree to keep the India-Pakistan dispute out of Afghanistan's bilateral relations with both, and have agreements on both sides to cease supporting or harboring violent opposition movements against each other. The report concluded that the United States, NATO and the United Nations must agree to send a common message to Islamabad: that the persistence of Taliban havens in Pakistan is a threat to international peace and security that Pakistan must address immediately.[91]

Most likely a great fear is that the madrasas are still in Pakistan producing more Taliban, according to *National Geographic*. The Jamaat Ulama-e Islam who support the Taliban are also there. If Pakistan were overtaken, one small strip on the southern border would be left. Musharraf may be willing to help the Pashtun in return for his country being left in one piece.[92]

Ambassador Amin speaks to the Pakistan situation:

> We think the reemergence of the Taliban resulted from the fact that the cross-border infiltration from the Pakistani side was not appropriately addressed. We also think madrasas, the religious schools outside of Afghanistan, continue preaching hatred and they continue financing and equipping and recruiting suicide bombers who were recruited from outside of Afghanistan. They get paid higher than the Afghan national army or Afghan national police forces.[93]

Hope in Regional Bilateral Relationships

In another 2006 report, the U.S. Institute for Peace said that the widespread perception among Afghans and others in the region that American interest in the country will fade quickly once its major objectives in the region are realized, could cause many Afghan and regional power brokers to begin "to hedge their bets" in supporting the Karzai regime. Pakistan and Iran offer Afghanistan its most imposing and critical regional bilateral relationships. Whether these countries cooperate or create obstacles for Afghanistan's recovery is greatly influenced by American strategic policies in the region. Afghanistan may not emerge as a regional crossroads for trade and resource sharing if the endemic economic and physical constraints and retrogressive political developments block progress toward the region forming a vital new economic entity. The report maintains that the emergence "remains a distant though hopeful prospect."[94]

As Afghanistan's journey moves toward stability and development, Haron Amin speaks of his country nurturing regional integration:

> Institutions ... not so long ago unimaginable, are taking root, and our citizens enjoy their freedoms and are optimistic about the future. Our economy is flourishing and Afghanistan no longer is seen by the region and the world as a pariah state, but it is actually seen as a land link in transit and a trade hub which is fostering regional integration. To put it in a nutshell, our people look better today. They are making the best of the opportunities that are offered and they are involved in local, regional and national development.[95]

2

War, Islam and Politics

The situation in Afghanistan provides perhaps the most clear and yet shocking and devastating example of the nexus between women's rights and international peace and security. Like "canaries in the mine," the well-being of Afghan women was a barometer for the overall conditions in Afghan society.[1]
— United Nations, Development Fund for Women, 2006

Politics and War

His Excellency Dr. Zahir Tanin, ambassador and permanent representative of Afghanistan to the United Nations, offers a direct look into Afghanistan in 2001:

> In December, 2001, I was in Kabul. It was winter and very cold. I witnessed the inauguration of Hamad Karzai as interim president, but first they had to find a place large enough that had not been damaged by the war to hold the inauguration. A place was found. That night when we went to the Presidential Palace, there was no heat, no electricity. A person had to find his own solutions to keep warm.[2]

In 2007, Ambassador Tanin noted the changes since then:

> Yes, much has changed in the last six years. By 2001, Afghanistan had become a failed state. Eight million Afghans had emigrated to Iran and Pakistan. Half of the middle class had emigrated from Afghanistan. The government was elected by the people, with Hamad Karzai as interim president. The constitution that provided women with equal rights was approved by the people. Roads were built. Schools and hospitals were built. Sixty percent of the children are in school. Women are

working in the media and in government. There have been changes in a woman's place in the family. Afghanistan has democracy and has a strong economy that has grown at double digits over the last years.[3]

He notes, "The possession of rights does not, at the same time, mean that we do not have some way to go." The conditions of women and men in a country that "starts to embrace democracy, starts from the establishing of rights." He comments that a lot has happened, but "at the same time, we have a comeback of the Taliban and increased violence are matters of concern."[4]

The hostilities between the Taliban and United States–led coalition forces that began in October 2001 have exacted a heavy toll on Afghan civilians. Although the international armed conflict formally ended when the Afghan Transitional Government took control in June 2002, the Taliban and other armed groups continue to target civilians. They have also been caught up in the crossfire in the ongoing armed conflict between the Afghan army and foreign forces and the Taliban and other armed groups opposed to the Afghan government and presence of foreign troops. "Both sides have committed serious human rights abuses and violations of international humanitarian law — the 'laws of war' — resulting in the deaths or injury of Afghan civilians," Amnesty International reported in April 2007.[5]

The Taliban have been responsible for hundreds of civilian deaths. According to the Afghanistan Independent Human Rights Commission, approximately 600 civilians were killed or wounded in the first seven months of 2006. Around 70 percent of these casualties were linked to Taliban attacks.[6]

In December 2007, a leaked UN map demonstrated that almost half of Afghanistan is too dangerous for aid workers to operate in. From 2005 through 2007, most staff have withdrawn from the southern half, leaving or scaling back development projects in rural areas. They moved to work in the less risky northern areas. This interference with the rebuilding projects is exploited by the Taliban. According to the unpublished map, security has markedly deteriorated since 2005 compared to a similar map from March 2005.[7]

In 2007, violence has risen 27 percent with a 39 percent increase in attacks in eastern Afghanistan, where most U.S. troops engage and a 60 percent rise in Helmand Province, where the Taliban resurgence has been strongest. Suicide bombings rose to 140, compared with five between 2001 and 2005. U.S. and other foreign troop losses and Afghan civilian casualties reached the highest level since 2001.[8]

In May 2007, the United Nations could not access about 41 percent of districts either on a permanent or semi-permanent basis. The security in the southern, southeastern and some eastern provinces is fragile. The situation in some western provinces is reported to be alarming. Civilians are victims of armed conflict on both sides and are allegedly used as human shields by anti-government elements. The UN Assistance Mission in Afghanistan reports 600 civilians had been killed in the military operations and suicide attacks through June 2007, either by government/coalition forces or by anti-government elements.[9]

The Taliban in 2008

In 2008, who are the Taliban? The Taliban are part of the insurgency in Afghanistan that includes al-Qa'ida, Jeysh-e-Mohammadi, Lashkar-e-Tayyiba and the armed political group, Hezb-e-Eslami. Amnesty International suggests "the term 'Taleban' has often served as a catch-all tag for armed groups or elements hostile to the central government and foreign forces. As a result, some attacks attributed to the Taliban by the media may have been carried out by al-Qa'ida, or by Hezb-e-Eslami, headed by Gulbuddin Hekmatyar. Hezb-e-Eslami and al-Qa'ida oppose the international intervention."[10] Other identifiers ascribed to the Taliban sometimes include local warlords, criminal gangs involved in the drugs trade or private individuals.

The Taliban are primarily Pashtuns from southern Afghanistan and from those living across the border in Pakistan in the Northwest Frontier Province and the Federally Administered Tribal Areas. In these regions and in parts of Baluchistan, the majority people are Pashtun and have in common the same history, norms and religious beliefs as their Afghan counterparts. Many of these Pashtuns do not recognize the Pakistan-Afghan border and cross it at will. In addition, Pakistan appears tolerant of Afghan Taliban and local Taliban fighters in its border regions. According to Amnesty International, local and Afghan Taliban fighters, "have reportedly regrouped and resupplied from bases in these regions, directing attacks in Afghanistan from these strongholds, in many instances with little interference from the Pakistani authorities."[11]

The Taliban's core fighters number 5,000 and part-time fighters total 10,000. Their government consists of a 33-member council (Rahbari Shura) headed by Mullah Omar. In 2003, Omar created a ten-member council of commanders to lead Taliban military operations in Afghanistan. The council consists of members of the older Taliban leadership who led campaigns against U.S. military operations in 2001–02, newer fighters recruited from religious seminaries or madrasas in Pakistan, and a small portion of foreign fighters that includes Arabs, Chechens and Iranians. The Taliban's financial support comes from regional supporters, wealthy donors from the Persian Gulf states, the illegal drug trade, ransom from kidnappings, proceeds from smuggling goods, and coercion of supporters in southern Afghanistan.[12]

Alarming is the *Guardian Unlimited*'s October 2007 description of the Pakistan Taliban who are giving birth to a wild and lawless new state in a strip of territory across Afghanistan and Pakistan. In this territory, warlords struggle for control and Islamic militants swarm in, fueling a growing conflict in the front line of the War on Terror. Jason Burke writes,

> What emerges is a picture not of a single movement or insurgency called "the Taliban," but of a new state without formal borders or even a name, a state that is currently nothing more than a chaotic confederation of warlords' fiefdoms spanning one of the most critical parts of the world and with the potential to escalate into a very real presence — with devastating consequences for global security.[13]

The violence is more complicated than saying that the Taliban regrouped after 2001, or that al-Qa'ida's Osama bin Laden and his key supporters are helping the Taliban advance their way back to power in Afghanistan, and even worse, helped them progress toward seizing power in nuclear-capable Pakistan. The conflict has no defined fronts and the tactics are confusing. On the one hand, it resembles nineteenth-century anarchists and trench fighters on the Western Front in 1916 who threw dynamite. On the other, it resorts to state-of-the-art twentieth-century warfare. This chaotic quasi-state has been in the making since the war against the Soviets thirty years ago. It may take as long or longer to break it up.[14]

"The war in Afghanistan is as much about perception as it is about conflict," National Public Radio states.[15] In 2007, more died in violence from terrorists than at any time since 2001. Battles were fewer, but far bloodier. Because of the NATO, United States and Afghan troops, Afghanistan is safer, but Afghans fear the insurgents will ultimately win. About half the country is unsafe due to the insurgency, and only about one-third is controlled by government. While the Western nations debate how long their troops should remain, reigning chaos is fertile ground for the Taliban. Thus, the Taliban's hit-and-run strategy permits militants to advance their fight and the drug dealers to increase their activity. Resurgent Taliban activity did not just happen in 2007, according to U.S. General Dan McNeill, commander of NATO coalition forces.

An identification of corpses killed in the fighting has confirmed the belief that bin Laden's al-Qa'ida has rebuilt a version of the terrorist infrastructure that existed in Afghanistan in the late nineties, reports Burke. Training camps do not lack volunteers and the militant presence is international in Pakistan areas. According to a UN report, the suicide bombers in Afghanistan are a result of recruiting and training that happens in Pakistan. Pakistan finds the situation complicated by the area having no tax collection, justice system or police force. Additionally, terrain is difficult, intertribal violence prevails, and mullahs of the hardline Deobandi traditional school of Islam form the private militias of the Pakistan Taliban. Along with warlords, they have been successful in keeping government authority from their territory and in laying the foundation for a state without borders or flags.[16]

The UN report states that analysts differ over the links between the two wings of the Taliban. Some believe that Afghan Taliban are not interested in gaining territory, and consider Pakistani Taliban a burden. Others believe the situation is too complex to draw that conclusion; for example, funding is received from Afghanistan through taxes, opium sales and wealthy sympathizers. Weapons come from Pakistan factories. Their short-term goals may differ, but long-term aspirations are shared.[17]

A recent book, *Koran, Kalashnikov, and Laptop: The Neo-Taliban Insurgency in Afghanistan*, suggests that, unlike the old Taliban movement of 1994–2001, the new insurgents have less orthodox attitudes toward imported technologies like video production. By 2005, some district commanders had laptops, despite the scarcity of electricity. The new Taliban have no misgivings about taking advantage of free-market principles for military operations. Because of their willingness to use new technology, they also use it to manipulate the media. In addition, they protect opium traffickers' escorts in exchange for favors and pay non-hardcore members by piecework, for example, by firing a rocket or carrying out an assassination. By late 2006, commanders were becoming less strict in enforcing the Taliban's moral codes.[18]

Taliban Constitution

The Taliban's constitution makes clear the limits of the Taliban's acceptance of international law, according to Amnesty International. The constitution states, "The Islamic Emirate of Afghanistan supports and upholds ... the Universal Declaration of Human Rights and other accepted treaties, as long as they do not contravene Islamic doctrine....."[19]

The Taliban have consistently said that their policies comply with Islamic law and Afghan culture, and thus are not open to question. The Taliban maintain that there is no difference between the armed people who are fighting against them and civilians who are cooperating with foreigners. Although international humanitarian law forbids targeting civilians, the Taliban do not distinguish between military targets and civilians or civilian objects, such as school buildings.[20] Examples of the sanctioning of targeting and killing of civilians are found in Rule 25 pertaining to teachers who do not teach according to Islam and in Rule 26 that suggests that NGOs and humanitarian workers may be targeted should they come to the country under the rule of infidels.[21]

To aid understanding of the Taliban's purpose, Max L. Gross, who served as dean of the School of Intelligence Studies, Joint Military Intelligence College, Washington, D.C., writes that some of the documents of al-Qa'ida and the Taliban appear to resemble the policy of the 1996 Malaysian leadership of the Jemaah Islamiyah conceptualized wholly in Islamic terms. The first of seven principles is "that establishment of religion requires the establishment of an Islamic state."[22]

Politics and Islam

The concern about Islam for U.S. intelligence personnel and national policy makers is with its political aspects rather than its spiritual or religious elements, writes Gross. The political aspects assumed a new importance since the 1979 Iranian revolution and especially since the attacks on the United States on September 11, 2001.[23]

Gross makes the distinction between statist Islam and civil Islam. Statist Islam, the traditional view that religion and politics are inseparable in Islam, appears to be on the rise. Gross writes, "In this view, there can be no security for Islam or the Muslim peoples without the protection of an Islamic state, one in which Islamic law (Shari'a) is the law of the land and is effectively administered by competent authorities."[24]

Statist Islam may fail because it is out of step with the pluralism movement of our age. When information comes from many places, ideas are challenged and truth remains elusive. Ultimately, Gross says, Muslims may find, "that the high values of Islam are more effectively maintained in an environment in which freedom of religion is guaranteed rather than one in which religion is coerced."[25] In Afghanistan, statist Islam and civil Islam are engaged in a struggle to dominate the government. Currently, civil Islam dominates.

Human Rights Reports

According to Amnesty International, the resurgence of the Taliban filled a void left from human rights violations by the Afghan state forces and foreign forces. First, between 2001 and 2004, the Afghan and foreign forces's detention of men, often the principal breadwinners, often left family members in poverty and destitute. These detainees amounted to hundreds of men. In many cases, the forces did not respect their human rights, including guarantees of due process. The detainees were tortured and given other ill-treatment, and at least eight of them died in U.S. custody.[26]

Second, the state-building process following the overthrow of the Taliban and the Bonn Agreement in December 2001 failed, in part caused by weak and corrupt institutions such as the Ministry of Interior, the judiciary and the police force. The way these institutions functioned resulted in a security gap across Afghanistan.[27]

Last, the government's harsh campaign to end opium production without adequately providing substitute employment led to opposition that created another avenue for Taliban infiltration. These three situations combined with young men's discontent with foreign intervention or being coerced into joining the Taliban militia provided a return to Taliban activity. Afghanistan is one of the world's poorest countries. A Taliban fighter earns about U.S.$300 a month compared to an Afghan soldier's monthly salary of around U.S.$100.[28]

The Human Rights Watch *World Report 2007* expressed discontent about events in 2006. The report explains that the Afghan government "took several steps that weakened the already weak government commitment to women."[29] First, in June, Karzai sent the Afghan parliament a proposal for reestablishing the Department for the Promotion of Virtue and the Prevention of Vice. Under the Taliban, it had established a record of arbitrary and inhumane abuses of women and girls. At the time of this report, the National Assembly had not debated the proposal. Professor Abdul Raheem Yaseer maintains that the Department for the Promotion of Virtue and the Prevention of Vice is now very, very different. It is like it used to be before the war and before the Taliban and during the period of the King and before that. He explains that the department

> is reestablished, but in a different nature. It is not like the extremist Taliban. Some kind of religious discipline is needed in every society. Otherwise people will ignore religious values and get too much involved in material life. They have to be reminded by the families, by the religious leaders, by the religious schools and religious institutions. It happens that there is a ministry of justice or there is a ministry of hajj who would like to keep people under control, because the provocation for going out of norms, like these movies and pornographic [media], music videos and magazines and papers infiltrate in the country and especially mislead the young generation of women and men. So, the schools have religious subjects. But the schools have so many responsibilities that they cannot concentrate on the religious affairs and keeping people within the tradition and culture and social values. That department was reestablished but its nature is totally different. Nothing is imposed but it provides guidance and training and consultation. There is nothing like the Taliban getting in the back of a pickup and stalking women on the street and beating them with wire cable.[30]

Human Rights Watch reported that in November 2007 parliament had begun debating the possibility of closing the Ministry of Women's Affairs. Professor Yaseer said that the Ministry was not closed and explained the reasons behind the debate:

> The reason is [that] the parliamentary election was done according to the Constitution and according to the democratic process. So, a lot of criminals and fanatics and extremists could win votes by using money and having the resources. They got into the Parliament. The Parliament is not clean. In the Parliament, there are lots of these bad elements. They could be Pakistani agents, [or] other agents.... They are known characters. There have been a lot of complaints and criticism about them, but they are former criminals, former commanders, former party leaders and they are all sitting there. They give the government a hard time for giving women more rights. They give speeches for publication. They have free media. They raise their voices against these kinds of modernization. Therefore, they have been trying to eliminate the Ministry of Women Affairs. They don't ... value ... women. They don't want them to gain power. They don't want them to have any rights. So they do these kinds of things.[31]

Human Rights Watch reported that Karzai failed to adequately implement the Transitional Justice Action Plan, a five-year process to gather information about Afghanistan's legacy of warfare and violence and to consider methods of achieving accountability. In December 2005 the cabinet approved the plan, but it gave way pending the required presidential announcement. The Taliban and other antigovernment forces used the government's failure to confront warlords in the government to gain public support and discredit Karzai's administration and its international backers.[32]

Ambassador Amin explains this complex phenomena by first clarifying the official position of the Afghanistan government:

> We believe that our people recognize the need for Afghans to put behind the case of conflict as a dark chapter in that the international community prefers peace over justice. Our government's position remains unchanged about the Transitional Justice Action Plan. We attach great significance to a South African style truth-and-reconciliation commission and tribunal. We also at the same time strongly support the right of any individual to come forward and seek justice against any individual group or entity who has committed the crimes of war or crimes against humanity. But we also believe that the current security situation in parts of the country does not allow for a comprehensive and total transitional justice.[33]

Amin further clarifies what is meant by transitional justice.

> Step number one: Let us put this chapter of war behind us as an evil, dark, ominous, bleak chapter. That's number one. What do I mean? For twenty-three years, hundreds of thousands of people slaughtered hundreds of thousands of people.... [I]f Afghanistan was invaded by the former Soviet Union and currently the heir to the former Soviet Union is Russia, and if Russia and Soviets killed millions of Afghans, why do the international community tribunals not take Russian leaders to justice.[34]
>
> Our question is why are they still part of the Security Council? Why should they be part of the Security Council? What about those soldiers and generals that came and murdered millions in Afghanistan? What about the country that came and created an upheaval and wreaked havoc on all of Afghanistan?[35]

"Number two: If we do transitional justice, it has to be equally, across the board, all ... across Afghanistan in every ethnic group,"[36] says Amin. He explains by citing Abraham Lincoln's legacy after the American Civil War:

> Lincoln did not discriminate against any individual that had fought in the war and he did not say even for them to surrender their guns. He said to go to their fields and build lives. For us, the most important thing was not to seek vengeance or justice, it was to seek peace. And when you seek peace, it means you let go of the past. What was important for Afghans was to let go of twenty-three years of brutality. Now, if the argument is, so and so last month cut so and so; let's bring him to justice. The person is brought to justice and he says so and so killed my cousin two decades ago. So you bring the other person to the courts, and they say last year the servants killed my cousin or my brother and so on and so on. So, all you've got is a vicious cycle of individuals avenging others.[37]

Amin concludes his remarks on transitional justice by demonstrating how the interrelationship of the first two steps he describes creates the third, that it has to be done. "If you cannot do number one and if you cannot do number two, then let's make it such that any individual who has been wronged, that has a case, [can] come and bring it to the court's attention and ... take anyone to court, whoever has committed a crime: crimes of war, crimes against humanity, crimes against individuals, whatever, whatever. And so that is plausible on an individual basis."[38]

Political, Economic and Security Vacuum

Because the Taliban have taken advantage of a political, economic and security vacuum, they have gained de facto control over large strips of territory in the south and the east of Afghanistan. Reports indicate that attacks are growing near the outskirts of Kabul and in centers in the northwest along the border with Iran and Turkmenistan. The insurgency gained ground in 2003. The resurgent Taliban's tactics consisted of suicide attacks, improvised explosive devices, assassinations and beheadings.[39]

UNICEF reported in October 2007 that the danger to children by the continued fighting is greater now than it has ever been since the war began in 2002. "In the first six months of this year, 44 schools have been closed in Afghanistan — either as a result of direct attacks or else intimidation of parents and teachers,"[40] according to Martin Bell, UNICEF ambassador. The greater use of airpower by NATO, militant bombings and Taliban suicide attacks kill bystanders, including children. Some Taliban attacks are directly on schools to kill girls they believe should not attend.

On November 6, 2007, the deadliest suicide bombing in Afghanistan since 2001 led Afghan President Hamid Karzai to say, "This heinous act of terrorism is against Islam and humanity ... [and was committed by] the enemies of peace and security,"[41] a phrase often used to describe militant Taliban. The Taliban denied involvement. The death toll in the suicide bombing north of Kabul was about forty-one, including six members of parliament. Eighty-one were wounded, half of whom were school children who were lined up to meet the lawmakers. In the past, Taliban bombers have killed regional governors, but never so many public figures at once.

Reports of this incident vary, but the UN issued a report that was not endorsed, that said school children suffered most from the bullets of lawmakers' bodyguards. The report of the UN Department of Safety and Security stated, "Regardless of what the exact breakdown of numbers may be, the fact remains that a number of armed men deliberately and indiscriminately fired into a crowd of unarmed civilians that posed no threat to them, causing multiple deaths and injuries."[42]

One day earlier, on November 5, 2007, the UN General Assembly had condemned the increasing violence and terrorist activity by the Taliban, al-Qa'ida and other extremist groups. The resolution stressed the "urgent need" to address the violence, indicating strong international backing for Afghanistan at a difficult time.[43] Insurgent violence was at its highest level since 2001 and suicide attacks were on the rise. Insurgency-related deaths in 2007 surpassed the 5,000 mark and a UN report found that the attacks had risen by 20 percent. Another UN report found that Afghanistan has averaged 550 violent incidents per month in 2007, up from 425 in 2006. An Associated Press count of insurgency-related deaths numbered 5,086 as of October 2007, up from 4,000 in 2006, and the most annual deaths since the invasion. The AP's count numbered more than 3,500 militants among the dead, and more than 650 civilians killed either by militant violence or U.S. or NATO attacks. Almost 180 international soldiers died in 2007, including 85 Americans, a slight decrease from 2006 of about 90 U.S. soldiers.[44] Taliban insurgents carried out 103 suicide bombings in Afghanistan in the first eight months of 2007, a 69 percent increase over the same period in 2006, according to a September 2007 UN report. These attacks killed more than 200 people, 80 percent of them civilians. This number is much higher than the 17 in 2005 and 123 in 2006.[45]

Casualties erode public trust, Louise Arbour, UN High Commissioner for Human Rights, said after visiting Afghanistan in November 2007. Half of the 1,200 civilian deaths were caused by international and Afghan troops. Still, she said that "public opinion was clear — there was a higher expectation of international forces [than insurgents] to do everything possible to avoid killing or injuring civilians."[46] She stressed giving adequate compensation to the victims and their families.

Include in this mix of violence the effect of private contractors on Afghan society. Estimates on the number of private security personnel in Afghanistan number over 10,000 for registered groups alone. The U.S. Department of Defense employs 1,000 security contractors, and the Department of State and the government of Afghanistan also hire them. This number is lower than those employed in Iraq, Carl Robichaud writes, "but it comprises a substantial military presence for Afghanistan. If this figure is accurate, private security personnel outnumber the troop contribution of every nation but the United States, and are almost a third the size of the Afghan National Army (estimated at around 35,000)."[47]

Number alone does not portray the implications of these forces. Who composes these private security forces gives a more complete picture. Because they consist of mostly Afghans, former combatants from mujahedeen militias, reliance on them has had the ruinous outcome of sustaining and empowering some of the nation's most irresponsible actors. Barnett Rubin argues that security contractors "have hired, armed, and trained militias that were supposed to be demobilized and disarmed, enabling them to persist and profit as part of the 'private sector,' awaiting the spark that will set off another civil war."[48] Rubin maintains that reliance on these sorts of actors is "corrupting the Afghan police and administration."[49] Yet the Ministry of Interior does not have the means to replace the protection guaranteed by private companies.

The November 2007 UN resolution "also backed the Afghanistan Compact, a five-year blueprint adopted by the Afghan government and the international community in January 2006 to help rebuild the country's government institutions and promote the rule of law, human rights and national reconciliation."[50] The success of this blueprint will be part of Afghanistan's success as a country. I interviewed Ambassador Tanin during the same week that the UN resolution was passed. According to Tanin, if there is security, "there is a window of opportunity for all Afghans to go in the right direction. Most societies would be created by design. As soon as we are able to establish institutions that are needed for the country, that will help. But it's a struggle."[51]

Tanin explains that there are countries that help Afghanistan, but the violence from Afghanistan's enemies is the downside:

> Since 2005, in some parts of Afghanistan, in the southern part of Afghanistan, in the eastern part of Afghanistan, there have been increasingly violent attacks: suicide bombing, roadside bombings, attacking children, women, bystanders. Not only people but also the institutions. We build a school, they burn it. We build a hospital, they burn it. So Afghan institutions and Afghan people are under attack in some parts of Afghanistan. The druglords, the warlords and people in neighboring countries don't want to see a stable Afghanistan. So we have big contributors like the United States of America, like Europe and other countries who would like to see a stable Afghanistan, but we have enemies who would like to destroy what we would like to do.[52]

Anne Cubilié writes that civilized countries repeatedly and willingly take part in activities that undermine civil society and the rule of law "when mobs or the state judge it to be in their best interests."[53] Deniz Kandiyoti explains that when dealing with situations of conflict and chronic political instability, we have to depart from the hallmark of "statehood." Statehood meaning there is an "existence of a viable apparatus of governance that may support or hinder women's rights and that may, ultimately, be held accountable to its citizenry. Even in the numerous cases where states fail to deliver welfare or democratic means of political representation to their population, a coercive apparatus with the monopoly of violence (the army, police and security services) remains the hallmark of 'statehood.'"[54] Our political lexicon now includes "failed states," referring to countries war torn and filled with internal strife, with collapsed, decayed or vestigial apparatuses of governance, and political economies dominated by criminalized networks involved in illicit trade in arms, narcotics and primary commodities.

Tanin describes Afghanistan as a country that was a failed state that is now better. "I say this, that we know what to do ... [remembering] when Afghanistan had no army, no police, no judiciary system, no central government ... or conditions for service. We speak about a failed state in Afghanistan ... There was no place to hope.... It was difficult to imagine how that can be decreed and how the people took it ... the [Taliban] had [no] conscience.... Kabul was not the place to be at that time [December 2001]. [People found] personal solutions [for lack of services such as] traffic lights and electricity."[55]

Afghanistan has experienced remarkable improvement since the country was near to being a failed state. Amin assesses the strength of Afghanistan's government to protect its citizens as stronger in 2007. "The Afghan government with its police force, with its militia force or army, is the strongest force in the country. Five years ago that was not the case. The government force was the weakest force and it was confined just to Kabul. Today, it has a reach within thirty-four provinces. It also has the ability to deploy forces throughout the country."[56]

The Afghan People

In the presence of war and transition, it is uplifting to note that the Afghan people have remained strong and positive. In September 2004, a nationwide campaign registered ten million Afghans who withstood threats of violence and voted in overwhelming numbers to elect President Karzai. In a March 2004 survey that was conducted in all but three provinces, the respondents were asked "Do you think that the elections will be free and fair, or do you think that they will not be free and fair?" Thirty-seven percent of 804 interviewed answered yes, that the elections would be free and fair, 60 percent said they didn't know, and 4 percent said that they would not be free and fair. In October 2005, 1,039 persons were asked, "Do you think that last year's elections were free and fair, or not free and fair?" Eighty-four percent responded that the elections were free and fair, 6 percent said they didn't know, and 10 percent said that they were not free and fair.[57]

Women's Rights in Conflict

Addressing women's rights in conflict and post-conflict situations presents "unprecedented challenges,"[58] notes Kandiyoti. Some believe that not enough attention and resources are allocated to gender issues. Amin says that the Afghan people have a desire to move forward. One reason that some people are not satisfied with the government is that people really have so many demands. A lot of times women put in a request so often that the Afghan government cannot deliver. It's very difficult for the government. They want change and they want it faster than it can happen.[59]

This concept is not new to Afghanistan. Dr. Lina Abirafeh writes, "Reforms repeatedly flood Afghanistan faster than the country can absorb them, should it choose to do so."[60] The reason, Abirafeh believes, is that women have received inconsistent signals from above throughout history, with enforced modernization at one time and at another time a reversion to traditionalism. Women didn't have much time to negotiate these opposing changes. As a result, women are left with a lack of clarity that came with traditional roles, yet they lack the resources to seize so-called modern opportunities.

The U.S. policy during the Soviet invasion of Afghanistan gave monumental support to mujahedeen groups, but only barely addressed human rights abuses, including extreme forms of gender-based violence under the mujahedeen. Aid agencies and NGOs were for the most part silent. The 2001 war, called by the United States "Operation Enduring Freedom," held the promise of addressing women's rights in Afghanistan. The low status of the country's women was invoked as a humanitarian crisis and was one reason given to justify military intervention. Since then, women's rights "have become implicated in the geopolitical maneuverings of powerful global actors," writes Kandiyoti.[61] Solidarity is problematic and it is against this troubled background that the nation building and claims on behalf of women should be evaluated.

Contradictions existed in the constitutional process in Afghanistan. While donor groups urged women's rights, lack of a stable political settlement between them and opposition groups such as the jihadi who interpreted the Shari'a conservatively, affected the process and result. The Bonn Agreement of 2001 endorsed gender sensitivity in government. As a result of the Bonn Agreement, the January 4, 2004, Loya Jirga approved a new constitution. Afghanistan had a new structure of presidential democracy and bicameral national assembly with lawful political representation of women.[62]

Some amendments were contradictory. Article 22 called for equality of men and women before the law and Article 23 an increase of women in the lower house, the Wolesi Jirga, from one to two in each province. Article 7 commits the country to abide by the UN Charter and various international conventions and treaties pertaining to human rights and discrimination against women, but Article 3 on Islam and constitutionality states that "no law can be contrary to the beliefs and the provisions of the sacred religion of Islam."[63] According to Kandiyoti, this article and one that declares Afghanistan an Islamic state, cannot be amended. The Supreme Court holds the power to rule that any law or treaty is not Islamic.

I asked Professor Yaseer about this contradiction and he explained:

> The religious transcripts ... the holy books, are considered to be divine rules. Human rights and the other rights are made by human beings and they are very functional, effective, and useful in societies and ... control societies with good education, societies with good systems of justice, like the United States and Europe. But when you apply these kinds of laws and rules, there are a lot of gaps in them when you take them to Afghanistan, Pakistan, [and] the Middle East because they are man-made laws and they have gaps, even in this society which is the

most advanced society. We see that when we watch the court scenes such as [in the] O. J. Simpson [trial]. You can see that the courts and the law could be manipulated somehow and there are a lot of gaps that are not covered. Muslims believe that their Shari'a law, heavenly law, is complete and is applicable in all situations and anything that goes against it, they don't accept it, no matter how on the surface it looks applicable, good and useful. They suspect gaps. Therefore, anything that resists or goes against the Islam religion, especially against the Qur'an and Hadith [are open to question]. I guess going against some the Islamic religious writings is okay, but anything against the basic laws, the basic beliefs ... is rejected. The constitution emphasizes that, too.[64]

There are a lot of people in Afghanistan who appreciate the international law. But there are some who resent it. The middle, the more moderate, more educated Muslims would like to see application of both into the life of this society. So the ministry and the government and the intellectuals are trying to adopt some of these international laws which are not totally against the basic beliefs [as] has been done throughout their history, in the years of the king, in the years of the republic, right now. There is a tendency to apply those things in the courts and things like that. But the fanatic elements always raise their voices against this.[65]

Haron Amin considers the passing of the constitution a remarkable milestone, "All citizens including women are guaranteed the right to life and liberty, to privacy and to peaceful assembly, to freedom from torture, and to freedom of speech."[66]

Women's Electoral Rights

Women were given the right to vote in 1963.[67] Afghanistan elected its first women to parliament in July 1965, the same time the present sovereign state established its first legislature.[68] The Inter-Parliamentary Union reported that the September 18, 2005, post-conflict election was important because the constitution guaranteed that seats were reserved for women.

The constitution signed and amended in 2004 includes a quota provision for each of the two main chambers. There are no political party quotas. For the Wolesi Jirga, requirements are that from each of the thirty-four provinces an average of at least two female candidates should become a member, which at a minimum should guarantee 27 percent women in the assembly (68 seats). For the Meshrano Jirga, the president appoints one-third of the members, and half of these should be women. A minimum of 17 percent of the seats must therefore be occupied by women. Election law also provides for quotas. In 2004, Article 22 (2) stipulated that the female candidates in each constituency with the most votes shall be awarded seats. Section 3 of the same article provides legal sanctions: "If there are not enough female candidates on the list of candidates to fill the seat(s) allocated to women in a particular constituency, the seat(s) in question shall remain vacant until the next intended Wolesi Jirga election."[69]

Over 300 female candidates ran for election. More than 52 percent of the voters, of whom 43 percent were women, voted in the 2005 elections for provincial councils and the Wolesi Jirga.[70] As of February 29, 2008, Afghanistan ranked twenty-sixth world-wide in percentage of women members in the parliament. Afghanistan's lower house, the Wolesi Jirga, had sixty-seven women out of 242 seats (27.7 percent). The 2005 election reserved ten seats for Kuchis, including at least three women, and reserved sixty-five additional seats for women. Members serve a five-year term. In the upper house, the Meshrano Jirga, twenty-two women held seats out of 102 seats (21.6 percent) for five-year terms.[71]

Social forces resist an increase in women's rights. A number of women won their seats on their own right and did not need a quota provision, but the majority (72 percent) depended on reserved seats. According to Kandiyoti, a goodly number of parties in the Wolesi Jirga are conservative/fundamentalist or Islamist and the jihadis are the most organized force in parliament. Women are associated with parties across the political spectrum and cannot be expected to function as a viable political group. She concludes that, in addition, women may not be in a position to avail themselves of their new rights on paper. Thus, "paper" rights are misleading because most women have limited contact with the state, market or civil society organizations.[72]

Haron Amin summarizes what he believes are some very remarkable milestones that have been achieved regarding the women of Afghanistan in addition to the passing of the constitution that guarantees rights and a certain percentage of seats for women in parliament. He says,

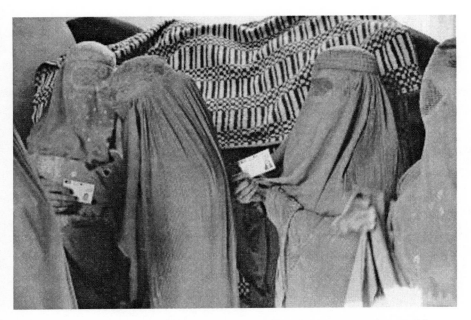

Afghan women stand in line to vote during Afghanistan's National Assembly and Provincial Council Elections, Kabul, Afghanistan, September 18, 2005 (USAID Photo).

Afghan woman dressed in a traditional blue burqa casts her vote at a women's polling station in Kabul on October 9, 2004 (AFP Photo).

Of the 500 members of the Constitutional Loya Jirga Grand Assembly in 2004, 102 were women. So that means more than 20 percent. Two out of the nine members of the constitutional drafting committee and seven of the thirty-five Constitutional Review Commission were women. More than 200 women participated in the 2002 Emergency Loya Jirga which established the transitional government. In the presidential election, out of the 10.5 million registered voters, 41 percent were women and there was also one female presidential candidate. In the September 18, 2005, elections for Provincial Council, in the Wolesi Jirga, or lower house, 52 percent of the registered voters were women.... The end result is that today we have ministers, we have ambassadors, we have lawyers, judges, business executives and so forth. Forty percent of Afghan teachers are women and 5 percent of the Afghan police are women. What that means is that the numbers are going to increase even in other institutions. But these were the beginning steps of Afghanistan in the context of what women have achieved.[73]

The UN Development Fund for Women lists other examples of women's increasing political participation. In 2005, women held 121 out of 420 Provincial Councils' seats, accounted for 26 percent of all civil servants, and increased their election registration numbers from 41.5 percent in 2004 to 44 percent in 2005.[74]

According to the Fund, women's political participation could be improved in these areas:

- Only one cabinet member is female (Minister of Women's Affairs)
- There were not enough women to meet the 124-seat quota at Provincial Council elections, and three seats had to be given to men
- In seventeen of the thirty-six ministries there are less than 10 percent female employees

In 2004:

- 87 percent of Afghans believed that women need a male relative's authorization to vote
- 35 percent of women believed they would not have permission to vote
- 18 percent of men admitted that they would not allow their wives to vote.

A session of the Afghanistan parliament, January 22, 2006 (Ben Barber/ USAID).

Nasrine Gross reports that the culture of war has brought elements that hinder women, including "the lack of rule of law, lack of knowledge of Islam, emphasis on ethnic traditions, and lack of social legitimacy for either women or modernity."[76] The trust the Afghans had during the periods of Kings Nader Shah and Zaher Shah is replaced by lack of trust and confidence and an unwavering fear of tomorrow.

Gross further describes the culture of war as the worldview of Afghan men having increased patriarchal behavior. A sharp line exists between men's and women's spaces, which decreases women's social, economic, political and cultural resources. Because women were not in the front lines or in the trenches, Gross says,

> The fighters, all men, developed a sense that life goes on without women. And today they feel that they won the wars without women, they can now build Afghanistan without women. In addition, this time around men are not mentors but rather competitors to women taking an office job; this is true even among many of the western-educated refugees who have returned. Men themselves are so thirsty for a job

and earning regular income that they don't understand that women also have a right to it. They think since according to Islam they have to support their wife and children, they should be considered first and foremost.[77]

Many of the problems women are facing are due to Afghans reverting to ethnic and local traditions seen as above the law, even the Shari'a, says Gross. These traditions are not Islam nor Afghan law, and include forced marriages for girls and boys, exchanging a daughter for a murder (which is called *badd*), denial of inheritance, marrying several wives without the knowledge of other wives, violence against women, and disallowing women education or work outside the home.[78]

In 2006, a female judge reported that trust in the legal system is weak and people within the legal system need training, "Otherwise there can be no trust."[79] Women judges have served on the bench in Kabul courts for the last twenty years except during the Taliban's rule from 1994 to 2001. In 2006, female judges seeking legal training in the United States reported that there were no juries in Afghanistan. Judges decide court cases. After reviewing hundreds of pages of information, judges write their decisions by hand, often in dim light because electricity is scarce. Parties to court cases often hold grudges, leaving judges fearing for their lives. The judges attributed the problem to police and military personnel still learning the legal system, to Afghans usually not understanding the law, to lack of employment opportunities and to poor court facilities that reflect the country's broken infrastructure. For example, water and electricity are not available. Courts share space with other agencies where judges do not have desks. There are no women's bathrooms. The courtrooms are crowded and judges often sit next to defendants. Hallways are very dark.

Dr. Sima Samar, who heads the Afghanistan Independent Human Rights Commission, reported in 2004 that despite improvements very serious violations of human rights still existed in the country, such as "arbitrary killings and torture, a lack of justice for victims, and violence against women [which] continued largely unabated."[80] The reasons for these violations included lack of law and order and security. Local powers or warlords are beyond the law and do what they want and are fueled by the lack of security. The rule of the gun takes precedence over the rule of law. Samar reports that past violations continue, such as arbitrary detentions, private jails, torture of prisoners and detainees, forced marriages and land grabbing. Access to justice doesn't exist because of cultural influences. For example, Samar says, "If a woman goes to court she is seen as bad and of ill repute."[81]

Most publicized was the shooting of Safia Ama Jan, provincial director of Kandahar's Ministry of Women's Affairs, and a well-known women's rights campaigner. She was shot in front of her home in Kandahar as she left for work September 25, 2006. The gunmen fled on motorcycles. Ama Jan was a teacher for over thirty years. During the Taliban regime, she ran an underground school for girls in her home. Since then, she established vocational training schools for women. The Taliban are suspected of Ama Jan's killing and a regional Taliban commander claimed responsibility to the Associated Press, but the claim could not be verified.[82]

Other problems include alleged human rights violations by those in government and problems of a transitional government that is made up, in part, of past criminals. Afghanistan does not have the capacity to deal with such crimes, and war crimes and crimes against humanity are not clearly defined in the constitution. These crimes would include alleged offenses by coalition forces.[83]

But Samar describes improvements, saying that the commission has been able to address 30 percent of the human rights problems. Because the people now recognize the office, they have somewhere to take their complaints. In 2001, no one could even mention the phrase "human rights." Some improvements have been made in the courts and prisons. For the first time, a national action plan on child trafficking was created with the help of UNICEF and Save the Children. In addition, the commission has addressed women's rights and entered prisons to visit prisoners.[84]

Examples of Improvement: Two Women

Improvements are seen in the struggles and triumphs of two women, Malalai Joya and Sahar Adish. Two award-winning films featured their accounts. Joya, a 28-year-old reformer and women's rights advocate, was elected to the Afghan parliament in 2005. In May 2007, the Afghan par-

In this picture taken December 19, 2005, Afghan member of parliament Malalai Joya leaves the parliament building in Kabul. One of the country's most high-profile woman MPs, she was kicked out of parliament on May 21, 2007, after she was shown on television saying her fellow legislators were "worse than donkeys and cows." The lower house of parliament voted by a large majority to suspend her until the end of its term in 2010 because, they said, she had insulted them (SHAH MARAI/AFP/Getty Images).

liament voted to suspend Joya from her seat. They cited a rule that forbids members to criticize each other. Featured in *Enemies of Happiness*, directed by Danish filmmaker Eva Mulvad, Joya is portrayed as an outspoken critic of the warlords and as one who endured threats and assassination attempts. She denounced the Northern Alliance military/political organization, saying it was just as bad as the Taliban. Joya is depicted on the run, moving from one safe house to another, in fear for her life.[85]

The second film, *Sahar [Dawn]: Before the Sun*, demonstrates the contrast of Sahar Adish's life in Kabul before the Taliban. Adish's parents were educated. Her mother was a teacher in chemistry and biology and her father was a geologist. In 1996 when the Taliban took control, Adish's mother secretly taught her nine-year-old daughter and other girls at home. In 1998, her father was seized, beaten and warned that he would be executed if the schooling continued. Upon his release, the family fled to Pakistan. In 2002, the International Rescue Committee relocated the family to Charlottesville, Virginia. In 2007, Adish was a 19-year-old student at the University of Virginia with plans to attend medical school.[86]

3

The Larger Context: Afghan Society, Islam and Family

Gender is defined differently in each conflict and in each context. In order to be sustainable, processes of social change must come from within.
— Dr. Lina Abirafeh, gender and development professional[1]

The Afghan Economy

When the Taliban were overthrown in 2001, Afghanistan was close to being a failed state. The political, social and economic problems were daunting. In 2008 there are signs that Afghanistan has changed significantly and continues to change even though old problems remain and new ones have surfaced.

Political progress and change have been significant and continue despite the resurgence of the Taliban. Social change has been influenced by the political, and in some areas the change has been dramatic, while in others it has been slowed by tradition. Economic progress has been substantial and in many ways is undergirding and sustaining the political and social change.

The developing Afghan economy has received less attention than politics and social issues, but the economy has contributed significantly to the country's stability.

The Condition of the Economy

In 2007, Afghan ambassador Haron Amin enumerated Afghanistan's economic accomplishments:

Today, foreign reserves run around three billion dollars. Exports are more than five hundred million dollars and the Afghan government has already spent 60 percent of its development budget compared to 30 percent in 2004 which shows the capacity of the government to spend money. The Afghan economy is to grow 13 percent this year, 2007. The Afghan currency has been stable. Collection of domestic revenues is very strong and the operating budget is being more and more secured from the domestic revenue.[2]

Afghanistan has seventeen national programs that consume a great bulk of the development budget, roughly five billion dollars. Of these, Amin says, the National Solidarity Program has been the most successful:

It has reached 15.6 million Afghans or 80 percent of [the] rural population in four years. It has put together about 20,000 community development councils, and what is significant is that a great number of the members of these community development councils are women. Millions of women are participating. They have a say in where canals are being built, where roads are being constructed, what farms need to do in corporate development. It's very important to highlight the fact that in many of these villages, an equal number of women show up for these councils that get together. In all, we can say what has been the trickling effect of just the national solidarity program. The notable achievements are: 28 percent of the rural areas have access to drinking water and improved sanitation, as compared to less than 5 percent in 2002; 11 percent of the children in rural areas have had the ability to go and enjoy newly constructed schools as a result of initiatives by these local communities. Women are a driving force saying that our children should live better than we.[3]

Eighty percent of the population has access to irrigation systems. Here again, a lot of the wives are supportive of their husbands and the only employment opportunity that they have is farming. Thirty percent of these people have electricity through hydropower stations or generators and ... 25 percent have access to markets through improved food networks. In a lot of areas in Afghanistan, it's the women who weave carpets, it's the women who [do] embroidery, the women who produce silk cloth, the women [who] dry fruits, and so on. We are looking at an enormous, huge number of the population, women being impacted by this development project.[4]

The largest infrastructure project is the ring road that links major cities. The Kabul-Kandahar span was finished in 2004; the Kandahar-to-Herat Section was near completion as of January 2007.[5] This road and other roads are being built to link remote farms to busy markets in cities.[6] Amin points out that

> the ring road will not only connect Afghanistan to itself for the export of goods, Afghan products, connecting cities, but it's also going to connect Afghanistan [internationally]. [I]n the U.S. or the UK, Afghanistan belongs to the South Asian Department; in Japan it belongs to the Middle East Desk; in Russia it belongs to the Central Asian Desk. So, what that means is [that] Afghanistan is a land-linking asset. It connects South Asia to Central Asia. It connects the Far East to the Middle East. Hence, the effect that we have or the comparative advantage for this country is that it is a land-linking or land-bridging country. Therefore, it needs to be looked at within that context and when we talk about empowerment of the country, we mean the empowerment of the people, and by that we also mean the empowerment of the women of Afghanistan who could in the future be serving in new sectors in Afghanistan.[7]

Amin elaborates on the progress of Afghan society in the context of communications.

> Seventy-five percent of the population has access to communication services. More than four million people out of twenty-five are using mobile phones. Every month the number of mobile users is increasing by 150,000. There are hundreds of thousands of women that are using mobile phones. I've seen them in Afghanistan. Fifteen Internet provider licenses have been issued. Right now at least a million people are accessing the Internet on a daily basis.[8]

Amin observes, "This is very, very promising. More than 50,000 jobs have been created because of the IT [information technology] sector.[9] Concerning the availability of electricity, he says, "By early 2008, 30 percent of the population will have electricity. And we believe that by 2011 or by the MDG (Millennium Development Goals), 75 to 80 percent of Afghanistan shall have electricity.[10]

The Challenges

FARMERS AND POPPY PRODUCTION: The thousands of Afghan farmers who turned to poppy cultivation to elevate their families from poverty quickly brought Afghanistan to the level of producing 80 percent of the world's opium and heroin. Some farmers shifted from poppies when the ring road and roads like it became usable and aid was forthcoming to assist them in producing wheat or other legal crops. The legal crops did not bring as much income, though, so, while in 2005 in Badakshan province, for example, strong leaders encouraged people to obey the law, in 2006 many farmers shifted back to opium production. A survey in 2004–05 of 1,843 Afghans in three provinces had 73 percent say that the cultivation of poppies for opium was unacceptable in all cases, while 21 percent said it was only acceptable if no other way existed to earn a living, 5 percent said it was acceptable in all cases, and only one percent said they didn't know or had no response.[11]

In 2008, NATO's International Security Assistance Force commander U.S. General Dan McNeill said that he expects to see another year of explosive growth in poppy production and that the multi-billion-dollar drug trade would fuel the insurgency.[12]

Refugees

Refugees continue to return. As they do, they help to revitalize Afghanistan, according to the U.S. Agency for International Development. By 2003, two million refugees returned from exile in Pakistan and Iran. In February 2004, their numbers reached three million. Four million people in all had returned by January 2007. The returning refugees have become the largest voluntary return in world history.[13] In December 2007, the UNHCR reported, "540,000 Afghan refugees ... are expected to return primarily from neighboring Pakistan and Iran.... About three million Afghans still live in Pakistan and over one million live in Iran."[14] Although the humanitarian situation is slightly improved in 2008, the areas affected by the war have produced internally displaced persons.[15]

The internally displaced often face the challenge of keeping warm and having enough food when temperatures fall to -26 Celsius (-15 Fahrenheit). Those people who moved to Kabul for a safer life, often find themselves living in tents and makeshift shelters in a windy field in Kabul's western outskirts. The severe winter of 2007–08 killed several hundred people and about 40,000 cattle, before the season was over, according to government estimates.[16]

Islam and the Family

Islam

In evaluating the position of women, a wide variety of circumstances should be considered. Islam is an important part of Afghan society. Islam must be evaluated within the context of all parties involved in conflicts and gender biases must be considered within the context of the social actors. Afghanistan's political situation is not due to Islam alone, but rather to past conflicts of parties that began during the Cold War fought by proxy in the country and continued after the coalition attacks. After the Bonn Agreement, the coalition continued their support of political groups to combat al-Qa'ida and the Taliban.[17] In addition to the conflicts of political groups, gender biases are inherent in kinship patterns, and family ties are eroded in poverty, displacement and a drug economy. Deniz Kandiyoti believes the gender biases are to be evaluated within the context of the diverse social actors in Afghanistan. Kin group and family violence to defend honor differs from sexual violence as a tool of war or, as in the case of the Taliban, social control. Interpreting Islam, therefore, cannot be simplistic.[18]

Nasrine Gross's book *Women in the Koran*[19] develops the role of women in Islam. Gross says that Afghans' knowledge of Islam is no longer from schools or their own reading but from mullahs and possibly illiterate family members. Afghans have a general awareness rather than specific knowledge of the Shari'a or the Qur'an. She believes that a deeper understanding is necessary to realize that Islam helps at peace time.[20]

The Ministry of Women's Affairs is working in many areas for women.[21] The ministry specifically addresses the root causes of the violence against women. The basis for solutions to violence is based in Islam:

> Respect, love and compassion with women were the characteristics and nature of [the] Holy Prophet who used to invite his followers towards kindness by saying: "Women are light and eyes in the house. Paradise is under the feet of mothers." Almighty Allah says in the Holy Quran, "No pressure" and by saying this He is stopping human beings from oppression and violence, especially against woman who is a mother. Islamic Shari'a and our national laws consider violence [a] bad-omen legacy from the ridiculous and indecent traditions of the man-dominant society's horrid and injustice.[22]

For the first time in Afghan history, women pray and read the Qur'an at a mosque in downtown Kabul, October 17, 2004 (AFP Photo).

Islam teaches that all types of violation against all human beings is a sin. The Holy Prophet (PBUH) says: "There is nothing dearer in front of Allah and His Prophet (PBUH) than faith and being moderate to others and there is nothing indecent in front of Allah and His Prophet (PBUH) than polytheism and violence against human beings."[23] The "PBUH" means, "Peace be upon him," short for "Peace and blessings of Allah be upon him." The acronym is a prayer applied as a suffix to the Holy Prophet Muhammad's name.[24]

On matters of divorce, the Qur'an says: "When you decided to divorce your wives then divorce them in the beginning of their monthly periods and count the period and fear Allah, your Lord. Do not force them out of their homes and they should not go out unless they commit a clearly visible prostitution."[25]

Violence is defined as a plague of faith that damages human relations, kills wisdom, reasoning and reflection; creates and can only survive with aversion; deprives hearts of love and affection, and a heart without love and affection is deprived of sympathy and mercy; a means for aversion with which the heart of a pious man runs out of sense of humanity; a phenomenon against humanity; and replaces human character with animal character.[26]

Family

During Nader Shah's era, 1929 to 1933, women's world revolved around family life. Men's lives were similar. Their worldview was small and directed to the local level. King Zaher Shah's reign from 1933 to 1973 brought peace and stability. Nasrine Gross writes of women's progress, "Among these changes, in my view, the women's participation in nation-state building that started in the 1920s and continued in the 1930s and on, and the women's emancipation that began in the 1950s and continued throughout stand as one of the deepest events affecting the culture of change."[27] She explains that her concept of nation building is that women began studying or working as paid employees outside the home. By the 1960s, the worldview of some parts of society changed dramatically. A culture of peace and trust was present, sure of its identity and religiosity. Women progressed mightily.

Since 2001, Gross says, "One of the most important problems in women's development is lack of social legitimacy for women in society and for modernity."[28] For example, no women or men without beards or professional office suits sit with leaders of Afghanistan when meeting with provincial elders and tribal leaders. Gross says the message is clear: social legitimacy does not lie with urban and modern Afghans. Further, the legitimacy is denied women when the president and most leaders are seen in public without their wives. In addition, national television sends a message that different ways of dressing are not acceptable when it features only women who dress with a scarf.

Ambassador Zahir Tanin is candid in his assessment of the complex factors that were either once a challenge to women's equality or remain so in 2008:

> Women had the distractions of the previous regime of the Taliban. They proved to be a distraction on women's freedom. The misery of women in a country like Afghanistan is related to their status they were put in caused by history, not only by the kind of regime like the Tal-

iban, but by social reasons, tradition, and the conflict situation [which] are also factors that contributed to their status. These factors must be taken into account. In Afghanistan, traditionally, the women have less rights than men. Sometimes there are those in Afghanistan who are not in favor of women.[29]

Tanin says that economic empowerment of women is key and must be taken into account because it also brings social agency.

> I think it is very important to see that it would be more credit to the advancement of women to empower women economically. That is very important. The government is also a process. Empowerment is not only an economic issue, it is also a social issue. On the one hand, you have to have laws and regulations that help women to become truly active in socialization. On the other hand, you have to create the conditions to enact the laws. That is very obvious. It is a complex situation. The rule of law is not in place everywhere. It is very difficult to see it in practice in all places.
>
> There are two Afghanistans. The Afghanistan of the city, the urban Afghanistan, and the Afghanistan of the villages, the rural Afghanistan. These are not the same with the way women are treated. One should take into account all these factors.[30]

The UN Development Fund for Women reports a high percentage of women (70 to 80 percent) face forced marriages and marry before legal age (57 percent). The divorce rate has also increased and beatings are the most common form of physical abuse.

The subject of forced marriages is of interest to many, including the government of Afghanistan. Haron Amin says,

> Everyone talks about forced marriages. Forced marriage has got an economic tangent to it. It has nothing to do with local customs or norms. Who would want to brutalize or subjugate his own daughter to a forced marriage had it not been for the issue of money? Even on the issue of narcotics or drugs, it is a matter of poverty.
>
> The government of Afghanistan through the minister of interior is currently printing IDs, identity cards for citizens of Afghanistan including women. These IDs will prevent child brides. The government initiative behind the printing of IDs is [that] the moment you have an ID, the whole child bride issue will be completely out. That's the initiative of the government."[31]

Table 3.1
Status of Women in Relation to Family Life and Gender

Marriage
— Women head 2.2% of Afghan households
— 70 to 80% of women face forced marriages in Afghanistan
— 57% of girls are married before the legal marriage age of sixteen
— The number of reported divorces increased from fourteen in 2005 to 158 in 2006
— There are one million widows with an average age of 35 years

Sexual and Gender–based Violence

The Afghanistan Independent Human Rights Commission registered 1651 cases of such violence in 2006, including:

558 cases of severe beatings
213 cases of forced marriage
106 cases of self-burning
50 cases of murder
41 cases of girls exchange
34 cases of rape

The Ministry of Women's Affairs registered 2,133 cases in 2006, including:

769 cases of forced marriage
1,011 cases of beatings
87 cases of murder
106 cases of self-burning
33 cases of rape

Source: "Situation of Women in Afghanistan, Fact Sheet 2008," United Nations Development Fund for Women (UNIFEM), http://Afghanistan.unifem.org/media/pubs/08/factsheet.html.

The Ministry of Women's Affairs in Afghanistan states that aid organizations should bear in mind women's family integrity. It states, "The culture of Afghans is based on honor and dignity, which is reflected through women's deeds. The gender roles are based on division of working place and authority among men and women. The position of men is general and social, whereas the position of women is specific and in the family. These two positions bear their respective roles and responsibilities."[32]

The ministry states that most males, especially in the rural areas, are content with gender roles. However, the advent of globalization and the effects of conflict have required women to become the guardian of their families due to the death of males. These realities bring pressure to bear on existing gender roles.[33]

But conflict also has its drawbacks in that lack of security restricts the progress of women. Women face forced marriage (which is often followed by suicide), child marriage, family violence, kidnapping of young girls, and threats. Reports indicate that in poor rural areas some families give or sell their daughters in fear of hunger. Human trafficking brings with it human rights violations such as forced labor, forced prostitution, and sexual exploitation.[34]

On some occasions practical needs of gender come in conflict with strategic needs, says the ministry. Female-headed families have the highest indicators in poverty and disability. In addition, they are landless, have fewer cattle, have little access to electricity, water and sanitation. Self-employment for women is very limited due to lack of loans and other banking facilities. "The burden of work on shoulders of rural women is very heavy. In addition to taking care of the family, they do agriculture, animal husbandry, and handicraft works,"[35] the ministry states.

Tanin believes there have been changes in family roles. The immediate changes are broader in that women can contribute in areas where women can work. Women want their girls to be educated. Under the Taliban women retreated, but now that women going out is increasingly normal, society is also discovering itself. But the Taliban are coming back because Afghanistan is on the verge of big changes.[36]

On the other hand, Tanin believes that the failure to implement women's rights is not just due to Taliban, but to social elements, tradition and the post-conflict status. He recognizes that in addition to security, tradition sometimes causes violence. Changing tradition takes time. He explains,

> Only by the instruction of the government [did women participate in government]. There were traditional areas where women played no role. There are areas where they started to be [allowed], like justice [and] defense. A sense of community is an important thing, with the IAS [Internet and cell phone service] arriving in Afghanistan and with TVs that are coming to their homes without their permit, and with the siding in favor of the rights of women. On the basis of my previous work and understanding, I know that women are more conscious of their rights, but we can't change tradition soon. What we inherited was

behavior that persisted generation by generation. If you would like to change them entirely, that will take time. A revolution can be done in one day ... but for culture, you need some time.

If you go to Afghanistan and travel over to other countries, you will find how Afghanistan is a moderate country that [is] changing her order and her sanity. There is a chance for women's work. Most men are ready not to prevent them from working. The tradition was that men thought that girls are only to get married. Let us say that one million people believed in this ten or twenty years ago, now you see that more and more people think that it is a good thing to give their daughters a chance to study. This is a change. Under the Taliban six years ago, men were told to cover their wives, not allow them to go out. What you see now is [that] women go out and the men are not against it. It is something that is becoming increasingly normal to see women out. This is not new. It is like a society started to rediscover itself as it was in the 1960s or 1970s. This is also recovering from something. There are some other limits. Millions of refugees came back from Iran and Pakistan and they brought with them some difference. Especially with people coming from Iran, because of social changes in Iran and the effect the revolution had, they are more conscious of the burqa. Then refugees came back from Pakistan and when people came back from Europe, they also contributed to that. We are on the verge of big changes including the attitude change. This is why the people like the Taliban are [trying to] stop the change. They do not want to allow capitalism to take root and democracy to take root.[37]

Tanin says, "I am aware of the poverty, of the burning — but we work to change."[38] He notes both the suffering and the progress,

Women again are suffering. When there is insecurity, the first group that is going to be deprived of education are girls. In some parts of the country where the Taliban try to destabilize the situation, schools are being burned. At the same time ... it is not only the roads that have been given attention. In each provincial center, there is a hospital. There is also a department for women, for gynecological [services], for obstetrics. There is a purpose. Of course, we have other problems. We need more doctors, more nurses, more medical technicians. Sometimes the international community also is not committed to this kind of assistance. So I am not ignorant of the problems. I am trying to compare the today's situation with yesterday's situation. I also try to be an idealist and see what we can do in Afghanistan. It is considerable the difference from the past, not only from the Taliban. We are much better in Afghanistan than ten years ago, six years ago, two years ago. The international community is now involved in many parts of Afghanistan to curb violence against women. But violence against women is caused by different treatments. Tradition sometimes is the main reason, rather than the Taliban or [like forces]. On the other hand, it happened to many and it is still happening that people sell their daughters, in a way. Sometimes it is a source of income for them to marry their daughters to a wealthy man. These kinds of things are illegal and evidence of

Opposite: Mother and baby at a camp outside Kabul. *Above:* Older woman at a camp outside Kabul (both photographs by Dr. Lina Abirafeh, October 12, 2002; reprinted with permission).

burning in hell. My government is concerned and people work for a better future for Afghanistan, work with the international community and with all willing people in the world to change the situation. I'm certain that we can change the situation, but I am not sure how long it will take. It may take five years or ten years to achieve something, but when we achieve something, there are a lot others to be achieved.[39]

The Ministry of Women's Affairs proposes possible measures to avoid violence against women. These measures include education and involving women in social, economic and decision-making activities. Also recommended is strengthening the legal system through establishing family courts, legal aid services, prohibition of forced and early marriage and of corporal punishment, Constitutional prohibition of violence, and regulations to prevent polygamy and to facilitate complaint hearings and legal aid services in line with national laws.[40]

Deniz Kandiyoti found mounting evidence that new patterns of relations are arising that are modifying women's roles in relation to indebtedness and dependence on local strongmen and drug traffickers. These variables lead to loss of community autonomy and encourage dependence. Daughters are sometimes given as wives in exchange for debt relief. Kandiyoti describes a study of indebted drug traffickers in Badakshan, where

> women rank next to land in the choice of disposable assets used to settle debts. Thirty-two percent of the traffickers interviewed reported selling a female relative (78 percent reported selling daughters, 22 percent sisters). The market prices of women ranged between $1,000 to $4,000 and the purchasers were drawn from all ethnic groups.[41]

Sharmeen Obaid-Chinoy, a CNN television reporter, found that often the influence of family on women and girls is harmful. Most disturbing is that some women burn themselves to death to escape the horrors of family life. Reliable statistics for the country as a whole on the actual number of women who burn themselves to death are not available, but the United Nations Population Fund reported in 2006 that thirty-six women burned themselves to death in Kabul, compared to eighteen in 2005. The number is believed to be much higher in the Taliban-held areas in the southwest.[42]

One reason girls burn themselves is to prevent being sold into marriage. Divorce is difficult to obtain and even if a woman or girl were to divorce, she would be an outcast. One girl interviewed had been sold at seven years of age and burned herself at eleven. The legal age to marry is sixteen. Self burning is increasingly common as families struggle to deal with the years of war.[43]

Families' efforts to cope is but one reason burning occurs. Women and girls burn themselves to make a statement and to escape family abuse. Few women seek or find the help they need. There is little evidence that the police follow up. It should be added that in not all cases do women or girls flee from a family quarrel that involved a male member. Sometimes it is the mother-in-law who is violent.[44]

Mothers-in-law also, along with husbands, make the decision whether a pregnant wife will go to a hospital to give birth. Obaid-Chinoy says, "Since the invasion six years ago, there's been little improvement. UNICEF reports that fifty pregnant women die each day. And that one in four children will die before their fifth birthday."[45]

Lina Abirafeh gathered anecdotal evidence during the period of 2002–06 and found "that the neglect of men in aid interventions has contributed to a resurgence of violence both at the household level against women and at the national level against the international community. It is possible to link the current increases in violence in Afghanistan at least in part to an insufficient understanding of men's needs and roles in Afghan society."[46] She argues that in order for gender roles to be sustainable, the social change must come from within. She also found that both men and women were uncomfortable with the prioritization of females.

Gender interventions have led to particular negative outcomes, writes Abirafeh, further destabilizing the gender order. Because the women feel misrepresented and the men perceive a challenge to their institutionalized patriarchy, men defend the gender order that is challenged with violence against women. Again, war and poverty has played a role. Men have lost their provider position and with it their identity. Abirafeh believes that gender equality is bound to fail unless men's lives are also made better and unless men are involved and supportive of changes. She concludes that making the shift from a focus of "women in development" to "gender and development" should not lead to a "men in development," but rather a reengagement of "gender and development" with a more healthy definition of gender.[47]

Tanin believes that urban Afghanistan is also changing for the better for women. He explains,

A few years ago, when you talked about the cities, you talked about the treatment of women in cities like Herat. Changes in Afghanistan have occurred in the provinces even though the province in the south of Afghanistan is a battlefield now. A few years ago, one of the women activists who was trying to help empower women in Kandahar was killed by the Taliban. The Taliban saw in her a threat to their campaign against women. The government and the economy are considerably changed. Some other programs are progressing. There is a big interest in education. At the same time, there are grave consequences of the war for millions of women in Afghanistan. Of course, the government takes responsibility. The responsibility may lead somewhere else. A good many people point to capitalism. The first thing is a move toward a new dynamic where women care about being in politics. Sometimes it looks symbolic, but it is not only symbolic. In the history of Afghanistan, for the first time, we have a woman governor in Bamiyan. It was not symbolic, because it has been two years that she has been working with the support of all people. In a post-conflict situation, and when you were in power, you might have been encircled by a former commander, by armed men. As a woman, how can you deal with this situation? How can you govern a construction project? How she governed in her office is that she is the one that nobody considers corrupt because she is a woman. She has a self-consciousness in the way that people look at her. So this is big proof. In the Interior Ministry and the Women's Ministry we have women officers and it is impossible to imagine that the mujahideen or the Taliban would accept them. There are a lot of sensitivities in the change. In the Communist-Leninist-regime era, there were women in institutions, but at that time it was not acceptable. Now we see that [it] is acceptable.... And the media is run or presented by young girls. You see a combination of things. Not only in the cities, but in the villages. Areas have been enriched in Afghanistan. The social relations are being changed. As long as we are able to strengthen the institutions, Afghanistan will emerge as a very different country. Afghanistan has always been [multicultural] in the sense and conscience of people. Islam is an integral part of our life. That has been working in a multicultural setting except the times that radical groups want to change that.[48]

Nasrine Gross observes that the strength of Afghan families since 2001 is that they provide a sense of identity. These aspects have not received the same media attention: strong family support, spirituality, the demand for equality, and the reemergence of women role models. After a very long period of insecurity, Afghans returned to their safe zone, the family unit. Gross writes that the family unit has "helped them withstand the unimagined misery, depravity and victimization."[49] She describes the family as,

> the most important institution of identity, socialization and moral support. This helps women feel secure about their actions in public; their public action is always with the permission of their family. Although sometimes they have to work hard to get that permission ... once granted, the family becomes their pillar of support, their defender and their cheering crowd.[50]

Islam has also helped the Afghan family cope. "They have no concept of life without God,"[51] reports Gross. This religious security is significant for women because they know that the Muslim God is egalitarian and judges men and women in the same way.

Specifically, since 2001 Afghan women have returned to social view. Girls of all ages are going to school, women are activists, teachers, office workers, ministers, ambassadors and governors, parliament members, a minister of women's affairs, and a woman presidential candidate who received more than 1 percent of ten million votes and came in sixth out of eighteen.[52]

Haron Amin adds that sports now includes women as well as men: "We have eighteen girl soccer teams; we have volleyball teams; we have badminton teams; we have hockey teams; we have cricket teams that ... are exclusively for women."[53]

Professor Yaseer at the University of Nebraska at Omaha sees improvements for women when he travels to Afghanistan. He summarizes the advancements:

> Women have achieved a lot of goals. They have become members of parliament, 30–40 out of 200 something. Women are representing their localities and their provinces and their towns. A great number of women have been working in government offices, in NGOs [nongovernmental organizations] and schools. So that is good. We have women ambassadors for the first time in history, in Bulgaria and Germany. We have a woman governor, for the first time, in the province of Bamiyan. Women have also been at the head of the human rights committee. So, even though they have not achieved all of the goals they have set for themselves, women have had goal achievement. Their rights

have been reserved and returned to them, though they are facing lots of challenges. There still are male members of parliament, fanatics, extremists, and conservatives, who are shouting and screaming and calling names, when women speak out in the houses of parliament. Some of the more vocal of the women receive threats of killing, imprisonment and all kinds of things. But, all in all, there [has] been great success for the women compared to the Taliban time and even before that.[54]

4

Education and Employment

We didn't know we were blind until we came to this class.
— Students at the Roqia Center for Women's Rights,
Studies and Education in Afghanistan[1]

Education

The progress Afghanistan is making in education is a bright ray of hope. The country's history shows periods of progress. In 2008 Afghanistan faces the positive problem of how to meet the needs of the great number of children, including girls, who have enrolled since the fall of the Taliban.

Schools from 1929 to 2001

During the Nader Shah's era, 1929 to 1933, Nasrine Abou-Bakre Gross's father was one of the few thousand second-generation high school graduates in Afghanistan. She writes, "There were no female high school graduates as girls' high schools were not yet in existence. The total number of educated people however was a little higher because a part of the aristocracy had studied abroad during their exile and/or work. There was a learned class of clergy as well and a number of Afghans were literate, having come through the classical, informal system of scribes (at home study of several major books, especially those known as *panj ketab* or five books)."[2]

During King Zaher Shah's reign from 1933 to 1973, education was one of several areas of progress. Due to a shortage of teachers, two of the four categories of recruits included girl students to teach lower grades and women who had some literacy and talent. The purpose of education was to teach girls discipline, new technologies, ideas and socialization in the larger society.[3]

In 1947 Kabul University was opened to girls. In the 1950s, schools moved from the palace and distinctly for the upper classes to all parts of town and for all classes.[4] In 1973, Gross estimates total enrollment in girls' schools was approximately 150,000. Although early marriage accounted for a high drop out rate, girls were entering the professions. By the end of the 1960s, though, the worldview in parts of society had changed dramatically. Gross tells her own experience as a student in Afghanistan,

> [M]y classmates and I, high school students then, imagined ourselves after graduation becoming women with jobs and careers outside the home. In the large cities, especially Kabul, there was also an acceptance of marriage by boys and girls selecting their spouse through social encounters although such choice still needed to be sealed through family sanction.[5]

Schools After 2001

ENROLLMENT AND ACCESS: Since 2001, many schools have opened. Gross reports, "Education is again commonplace, which creates a routine that tomorrow does exist and homework must be done."[6] Estimates are that close to five million children are enrolled in school, 40 percent of whom are girls. This number is the highest percentage of female students in the history of Afghanistan.[7]

The *Humanitarian Action Report 2008* gives a similar enrollment picture. Two million primary-school-aged children (60 percent) are out of school, with an estimated 1.3 million of them being girls. The Ministry of Education figures provided in 2006 indicate that 3,929 schools did not have buildings, 535 school buildings were damaged and 1,481 schools needed additional classrooms; overall there were 2,219 schools which had useable buildings. Access to sanitation facilities was as low as 12 percent.[8] The Afghanistan Ministry of Education reports that in 2007, 3,704 schools had buildings; 4,956 schools did not have buildings; and for 402 schools the building status was unknown.[9]

A teacher of accelerated education classes in Kabul, January 18, 2006 (Ben Barber/USAID).

Gross, who is the founder of the Roqia Center for Women's Rights, Studies and Education in Afghanistan, shares this picture:

> In 2007, I visited ten schools. Three or four were in Kabul and the rest were in the provinces. You have no idea of the conditions of these schools. I gave four of the schools twenty desks and chairs left over from my classes. That was like a godsend because most of the students were sitting on the floor. I saw schools with not a single chair. Children were sitting on the ground. I visited a high school in Mazār. The ninth grade consisted of 250 students who were studying thirteen subjects. Only one textbook was available. The principal was crying, "What do my teachers teach to these students? How can they make up lessons?" The teachers do not have enough money to buy a notebook for themselves. I took two boxes of notebooks for teachers. They all teach English and they do not have a single English dictionary. They do not have an alphabet chart, either for English or Pashto. They do not have a multiplication table, not a single map.[10]
>
> Even my third year students at the University of Kabul never had a map of Afghanistan, I had to teach them the map of Afghanistan and who the neighbors were.[11]

Gross explains that it isn't that textbooks aren't available in Afghanistan. Her findings reflect Oxfam's report of the need to restructure activities of the Ministry of Education.[12]

> The [U.S. Agency for International Development] printed fifteen million textbooks. The problems is that the government does not distribute equitably. Some schools get everything. Most schools don't get anything. To correct the situation, a well functioning Ministry of Education is needed because schooling in Afghanistan is public. Everything goes through the Minister of Education who should pay most attention to the daily operation of schools. Some problems stem from the fact that all ministers, not just in education, deal with their ministries in a political way. Whoever they like politically receive attention; whoever they don't like, doesn't receives any attention. The attention includes any need of the school, not just textbooks. The problems are hard to fix and are political in nature.[13]

The minister of education reports that there are not enough trained teachers, Gross says. In the high school that Gross attended, ninth graders are taught by twelfth graders. She says:

> We graduate every year 50,000 high school students. So why don't we make an army of learning, like the Peace Corps to hire these twelfth graders to be teachers at schools and at literacy classes. Afghanistan cannot absorb these 50,000 high school graduates. About twenty-five to thirty thousand of them get into the university and the other twenty-five to thirty thousand become unemployed and stay at home. Why not absorb them in a corps and give them a salary for the two years that we ask them to teach. You learn things and we learn things.

The *Humanitarian Action Report* underscored that incidents and threats against students and teachers continue. Thirty-seven attacks against schools, primarily torching and explosions, were reported in all parts of the country through August 2007. Attacks on female students and teachers resulted in at least five deaths and six injuries.[14]

In 2006, regional disparities existed, with girls representing less than 15 percent of the total enrollment in nine provinces in the east and south. High dropout rates affected the schools. In 1999, 74 percent of the girls in grades 1–5 dropped out compared to 56 percent of the boys.[15] President Karzai's speech to the Afghan National Assembly on January 21, 2008, acknowledged that the Taliban insurgency had deprived at least 300,000 children of attending school in southern provinces.

The primary school attendance ratio was estimated at 40 percent for females and 66 percent for males in 2000–06, according to UNICEF indicators. The school attendance ratio for secondary school attendance is lower, 18 percent for males and 6 percent for females.[16]

The Associated Press reported in 2008 that boys and girls are going to school in record numbers, though. About 5.8 million students, including two million girls, are now in class, compared with less than a million under the Taliban. Afghanistan's schools number 9,400, but only 40 percent are actual buildings. Sixty percent of classes are held in tents or the open air.[17]

Gross says the statistics show a downside:

> I am very worried about the schools because there are about fourteen million children between the ages of one and eighteen and about ten to eleven of these fourteen million children are school age. We still have 4.5 million children that are not in school. That means 50 percent illiteracy in Afghanistan, and that represents just the school-age children.[18]
>
> I am also worried about the girls' enrollment, especially in the Pashtun belt. In some places only 10 to 15 percent of girls are enrolled. That means that the women of Afghanistan are going to be mostly illiterate in the next generation. A World Bank study, not made public, found that the dropout rate for the boys to the sixth grade is about 90 percent; and for the girls to the third grade is 98 percent.[19]
>
> So, what will happen to the next generation of Afghans if we accept ... that the war and the calamity of Afghanistan was partly due to the fact that Afghanistan did not have a critical mass of educated people. Then we are surely not trying to create a critical mass with these statistics.[20]

Effects of the Taliban on Education

Professor Yaseer stresses that education is an area of improvement in Afghanistan in spite of the obstacles. He says, "Many, many children returned to schools despite all the opposition by the Taliban and terrorists against schools, [to] the opening of schools and education. They have burned a lot of schools and killed teachers, but many more students than before, almost seven million students, boys and girls, are now studying and going to schools, even though there are not that many buildings and facilities. The people want their children to study."[21]

Education Minister Mohammad Hanif Atmar reports that the Taliban strategy is deliberate, "to close these schools down so that the children and primarily the teenagers that are going to the schools — the boys — have no other option but to join the Taliban."[22] Since the Taliban recognize that educated Afghans will not join the militants, a closed school provides students with the choice of joining the Taliban or "to cross the border and go into those hate madrassas [where] they will be professionally trained as terrorists," Atmar said.[23]

The number of students and teachers killed in Taliban attacks has tripled in 2007, according to Atmar. Although overall education shows improvement, Education Ministry numbers demonstrate a sharp decline in security for students, teachers and schools in the south: "The number of students out of classes because of security concerns has hit 300,000 since March 2007, compared with 200,000 in the previous 12 months, while the number of schools closing has risen from 350 to 590."[24]

Atmar said that because of a community defense initiative, attacks on schools still open actually fell in the last ten months of 2007, to 98 from 187 in the same period of 2006. However, the Taliban had changed their approach to targeting students on their way to and from school or in other places where they gather.[25]

Emerging Standards in States of Conflict

Important to note is UNESCO's sixth edition of the Education for All *Global Monitoring Report* that assesses the extent to which worldwide dedication to a collective commitment to dramatically expand educational opportunities for children, youth and adults by 2015 are being met. This report lists Afghanistan as one of thirty-five of the world's fragile states. More than half a billion people live in these states defined for certain with poverty and stagnation that substantially increases proneness to civil war. UNESCO defines these states as ones lacking stability:

> International, civil and ethnic conflict, extreme and prolonged economic hardship, weak governance or high levels of inequality may cause

state institutions to weaken, fail or collapse. Affected countries could likely benefit from aid but do not generally meet the criteria of policy ownership and partnership required by development agencies. A concept of "fragile," "failing" or "failed" states has been emerging to describe such situations.[26]

The report states that there is not yet a global overview of Education for All achievement due to data limitations in countries excluded from the global EFA picture. These states which are in conflict, post conflict or otherwise fragile deserve special attention. These countries include Afghanistan, Angola, the Central African Republic, the Congo, the Democratic Republic of Congo, the Gambia, Haiti, Liberia, Sierra Leone, Somalia and Sudan.[27]

The thirty-five fragile states identified accounted for approximately 37 percent of all out-of-school children in 2005. Providing places in primary schools for these children is especially problematic. Data was not available for Afghanistan's number of out-of-school children.[28] Specific to Afghanistan, the report found high gender disparities, with the Gender Parity Index or the ratio between the female and male global Gross Enrollment Ratio (GER) below 0.90.[29] The report also indicated that significant gender disparities in access to education continue to affect girls in Afghanistan. The country, along with others, has made progress toward the reduction of gender disparities since 1999, but the female GER in 2005 was only 80 percent or less of the male GER.[30]

Unprecedented Enrollment

The UN Children's Fund (UNICEF) reports that school enrollment is the largest in Afghanistan's history. UNICEF has provided support to rebuild over 200 schools, supported the construction of nine teacher-training centers, and trained 50,000 primary school teachers.[31] The Afghan government's enrollment target for 2015 is 100 percent with girls' share of target enrollment being 50 percent.[32]

The aid agency Oxfam said in its report that enrollment has increased sharply since 2001. In 2006, approximately five million children attended school — an increase of 50 percent from 3.1 million students in 2003, and a 350 percent increase since the fall of the Taliban in 2001. But more than half of all children — almost seven million — are out of school.[33] The report indicated that Afghanistan needs to be able to cope with the unprecedented enrollment increase while at the same time generate demand for further enrollment, particularly among girls who continue to remain out of school. Children in rural areas have minimal access to education.[34]

Of the children in school, only one-third (1.7 million) were girls in 2005–06. Although overall enrollment has increased, at the primary level the gap in enrollment between boys and girls has remained fairly constant. At the secondary level, older girls have especially low enrollment rates, with 5 percent for girls compared to 20 percent for boys during 2005–06.[35] According to the *Afghanistan Human Development Report 2007*, the national average for attendance of children six to thirteen is estimated at 37 percent with enrollment in urban areas being higher, with about a 1:1 ratio of urban girls and boys attending. Cultural practices and access are the main reasons for the higher ratio.[36]

In January 2008, Afghanistan's Ministry of Education reported that in 2007 the student enrollment was about two-thirds male, 3,834,221 (64.44 percent), while 2,116,234 (35.56 percent) were female students. The

Table 4.1
Number of Students in Afghan Schools, 2005–06 and 2006–07

2005–06

Gender	Primary School	Secondary School	High School	Total
Male	2,769,163	348,934	143,087	3,261,184
Female	1,538,879	113,445	38,293	1,690,617
Total	4,308,042	462,379	181,380	4,951,801

2006–07

Gender	Primary School	Secondary School	High School	Total
Male	2,930,784	533,834	203,244	3,834,221
Female	1,738,326	201,863	67,900	2,116,234
Total	4,669,110	735,697	271,144	5,905,455

Source for 2005–06: "Free, Quality Education for Every Afghan Child," Oxfam Briefing Paper, November 2006, Table 2, 9, Oxfam International, http://www.campaignforeducation.org/resources/Nov2006/education%20for%20every%20afghan%20child.pdf (accessed November 29, 2007).

Source for 2006–07: 2007 Schools Survey Summary Report, January 2008, 12, 13, Afghanistan Ministry of Education, http://www.moe.gov.af (accessed March 30, 2008).

ministry also reports that in Islamic education, girls made up only 7.57 percent of the total student population and 10.08 percent of the technical and vocational students.[37]

The Challenges to Achieving Enrollment Goals

Although enrollment has increased 500 percent from 2000 to 2006, half of the children still do not attend school. The Oxfam report reasons that hope for Afghanistan lies with the children. "With the establishment of democracy, the main symbol of national regeneration [lies] in the dream of educating every child — boy and girl."[38]

COST TO HOUSEHOLDS: Challenges remain to achieve this dream. Oxfam notes poverty, informal end-user fees and other costs contribute to students not enrolling, but says the user fees have the most damaging effect. The government has been unable to meet the full costs of education because of the historic increase in enrollments. Thus, households are often forced to pay fees, which has in some cases resulted in children dropping out or being unable to attend school. Household expenditure for education on average is 188 afghani (Afs) or about 3.78 U.S. dollars[39] per month. The highest is at least eight times that in Kabul and Herat provinces, while the lowest is in the provinces of Badghis, Helmand, Nimroz, Sari-I-Poul, and Uruzgan where education may not be offered, where the populace is generally poor, and where strong cultural factors dictate.[40]

LACK OF EDUCATIONAL MATERIAL AND TEACHERS: Students in schools are faced with inadequate educational materials, textbooks, and teachers. A need exists for more teachers, particularly female teachers who represent 28 percent of the total. Oxfam reports that the number of teachers is between 140,000 and 143,000, shortage of 52,722. Funds are available to train only 10,000 per year. Only 17 percent of all teachers are professionally qualified — that is, have more education than grade 12. Teacher training centers number twenty-two.[41] UNESCO's report stated that high pupil-teacher ratios, above 40:1, leave teachers overcommitted to the point that the quality of teaching and learning suffers. In 2005, the worldwide weighted average primary ratio was 25:1, with developing or transition countries being higher. Afghanistan's is a high 83:1,[42] up 130 percent from 1999 when it was 36:1. The total number of teachers nearly doubled, but this was not enough to meet the need generated by a the greater rise in enrollments, including the influx of girls previously excluded from school. Extremely high pupil-trained teacher ratios of above 100:1 have occurred in Afghanistan, Chad, Madagascar, Mozambique and Nepal.[43]

Teachers are unevenly spread across provinces and they do not all receive the same wage. Estimates are that ghost employees account for between 16,000 to 20,000 teachers. These teachers may be teachers who do not appear for work, who collect only their salaries, or teachers who collect more than one salary if they are registered more than once. Afghanistan's Ministry of Education is planning a teacher registration to combat this problem. Only 17 percent of all teachers are qualified. Teachers are not paid on time and must pay a fee to receive their salaries. Out of thirty-seven planned teacher training centers, only twenty-two are functional.[44]

Budget allocation and spending in the education sector by various stakeholders remain largely uncoordinated and unclear. If this improves, most of these challenges can be met by addressing inefficiencies in financing.[45]

LACK OF SECURITY: Security remains a problem. While the number of girls in school increased quickly after the fall of the Taliban in 2001, only 35 percent of school-age girls were in school in 2006. The violence directed at schools hit girls' schools particularly hard.[46] Parents have been threatened with violence and death through Taliban night letters if they send their children to school.[47] The *National Geographic* reported that the effort to build schools is a doomed one because there is no security. In 2006 school attacks numbered 170,000.[48] The UNESCO report acknowledged that in countries of conflict or natural disaster, damage to the education infrastructure may be acute. "In Afghanistan, the burning and bombing of schools and the killing of teachers and students severely affected education provision in some provinces. In 2006, Afghanistan's president stated that 100,000 children who had gone to school in 2003 [and] 2004 were no longer attending."[49]

In 2008, the United Nations Office for the Coordination of Humanitarian Affairs described the situation:

At least 230 students and teachers have been killed and about 250 schools attacked by militants in the past three years, according to the Afghanistan Ministry of Education (MoE).

Owing to these attacks, over 400 schools remain closed, mostly in volatile southern provinces, denying education to thousands of students, MoE officials said.

Almost 70 percent of school-age children are not attending schools because of insecurity in Helmand, Zabul and Uruzgan provinces, Haneef Atmar, the Afghan minister of education, told a meeting in Lashkargah, the capital of Helmand, on 9 December.[50]

By 2008, the record violence of the previous year had killed 147 students and teachers, and closed 590 schools, nearly as many as the 680 the United States had built. The number of students and teachers killed in Taliban attacks tripled from the past year, to 147. The number of students out of class due to security concerns had reached the 300,000 mark since March 2007, compared with 200,000 in the previous twelve months. The number of schools closed had risen from 350 to 590.[51]

THE TALIBAN'S ROLE IN SCHOOL VIOLENCE: One source of violence is the Taliban who have a deliberate policy of targeting civilians. Their activities include killing teachers, abducting aid workers and burning school buildings. The Taliban's military rule book, or Laheya, explicitly sanctions targeting and killing civilians. Rule 25 states that a teacher who continues to teach after warnings from the Taliban must be beaten, and if he or she still continues to teach "contrary to the principles of Islam," the teacher must be killed. Similarly, a Taliban fatwa, or religious edict, orders the death of anyone who supports the U.S.-led intervention.[52]

Sharmeen Obaid-Chinoy found that the educated and outspoken women suffer as well as the poor. Nadia Anjoman, a poet who published a book in Herat, was killed in 2006. She refused to follow the Taliban's ban placed on women's education and had secretly studied literature with a group of friends.[53]

SOCIAL ISSUES: Social factors are also a challenge in education. As indicated above, poverty negatively affects school enrollment and the retention rate of girls. Education is free, but school uniforms and stationery are not. The loss of girls' income earning activities as domestic workers when girls attend school is of concern to poor families. These factors discourage poor families from enrolling their girls in school. The low marriage age also leads to low retention rates for girls. Another factor is the negative attitude of some parents toward girls' education, particularly on the part of illiterate fathers.[54]

LACK OF AID AND INFRASTRUCTURE: Other challenges to providing education are insufficient monetary aid and the slowness of rebuilding the infrastructure. Afghanistan experienced a bubble of financial aid from 2002 to 2003. Education is a central role of the government and it runs 97 percent of the schools. Progress on curriculum development, teacher training and system reform have been temporarily postponed.[55] Obaid-Chinoy found that in addition to some girls meeting resistance at home, aid has not always been forthcoming. For example, in the northeastern town of Talakan, progress and lack of progress coexist. Four thousand girls are able to study, but space in which to teach them is lacking. Sufficient aid has not arrived.[56]

Lack of facilities is particularly evident in rural areas and there is an even greater problem for girls' secondary schools. Lack of security, transport and distance keeps girls from accessing schools. Other problems include lack of water supply and toilet facilities.[57]

The Oxfam report indicates that reconstruction of the infrastructure is critical to increased enrollment. Seventy-five to 80 percent of school buildings were damaged or destroyed during the conflict. At the time of the report in November 2006, 1,100 schools had been constructed or rehabilitated by the Ministry of Education. From 2004 to 2006, the National Solidarity Program constructed 300 schools, and external organizations built 500.[58]

The UNESCO report cites a recent study of the behavior of some individual donors. The International Development Association and the United Kingdom tend to allocate their aid to basic education, based on education needs and poverty. Others, such as France, Germany, the United States and the European Commission, are usually influenced by strategic and political elements and a recipient country's absorptive capacity. In 2004 and 2005, Afghanistan, along with Bangladesh, India and Pakistan, received 17 percent of all aid to education. Likewise, the predominance of these countries in aid to basic education stands out. These same countries increased their share of total aid to basic education substantially.[59] From 2003 to 2005 Afghanistan, along with Ghana and Nicaragua, received aid in education from eleven donors.[60]

Afghanistan is among twelve countries that received well above the average per child for all developing countries. It is also one of thirty-two countries considered to be most at risk for not achieving universal primary education.[61] UNESCO states, "The case for continuing to allocate significant amounts of aid to all countries in this group is very strong indeed."[62] However, they also realize that how to channel this aid to fragile states remains a key question.

The UNESCO report states that renewing the infrastructure of destroyed schools is no easy task. Not only is there a teacher shortage, but also there is a shortage of builders, plumbers and other skilled workers. Afghanistan has experienced a tumultuous period of reconstructure and peace building. Rebuilding the education system has been a major effort. Several NGOs have assisted in providing access to education, especially for girls. NGOs first established community-based and home-based schools and then mainstreamed nonformal learners into the formal government system. The report clearly realizes Afghanistan's efforts

> In 2004, some 1.3 million girls were enrolled in government primary schools, a major accomplishment given that, in 2001, the number was recorded as zero.[63]

Literacy Programs

UNESCO reports that large-scale literacy programs, that sometimes include life skills in health and civic rights, livelihoods in income generation and farming, and/or equivalency education, are common, particularly in poor countries such as Afghanistan, Ethiopia, Nepal and Senegal. International NGOs and bilateral and multilateral agencies support these programs.[64]

ADULT LITERACY: UNESCO found adult literacy rates of below 50 percent in some countries, including Afghanistan. Improving global trends in literacy will depend on continuing to reduce the number of adult illiterates in heavily populated developing countries. Afghanistan is not listed as one of these eight high-population countries.[65]

UNICEF and its sister organization UNESCO hope together to increase adult literacy by 50 percent over the next three years. In 2007, 52 percent of Afghani men and 22 percent of women could read and write. The Joint Partnership on Adult Functional Literacy, an effort of the Afghanistan government and United Nations agencies, has reached an estimated 160,000 Afghans, mostly women. The majority of the program's tutors are women.[66]

Women's literacy is critical in addressing gender inequality. Afghanistan was one of the twenty-one countries out of 133 with a literacy rate for females less than two-thirds of that for males. Illiteracy rates are highest in countries with the greatest poverty. Likewise high rates are found in the poorest households and in population groups who are excluded from mainstream society such as ethnic minorities, migrants, indigenous people or the disabled.[67]

Professor Yaseer agrees that literacy for women and men alike is critical not only in assisting women toward gender equality, but is the key to social factors. He explains,

> There could be more training in education for the women because a great number of women, more than men, are illiterate. Also, chances of higher education and studies abroad are very limited for women and unfortunately, for study inside. There is supposed to be more effort put into literacy programs for women. Not only in the capital cities but in the provinces as well. Also, [there could be more] education for men [regarding] women's rights, educating fathers and husbands and brothers about providing opportunities and not being afraid of educating the female members of the family. The men need to have an open-mindedness for letting women go to school ... Education is the key for the solution of man and woman problems in Afghanistan.... [I]f there is not a university in the province that he lives in, [a man] can move to another place. But sometimes families are hesitant to have their daughters leave town, leave home and go to study. So these educational programs for women as well as for men are very necessary.[68]

ROQIA CENTER FOR WOMEN'S RIGHTS, STUDIES AND EDUCATION IN AFGHANISTAN: Nasrine Abou-Bakre Gross founded the Roqia Center for Women and named it after her mother. The center's purpose, in part, is to educate women at the grassroots level. Gross says of the program,

The same way that the modern world cannot afford to have the women of a society sit at home anymore ... modern society and especially a democratic society cannot afford to have its citizens illiterate. If you are interested in success in Afghanistan, you must be literate. In Afghanistan, over 90 percent of adult women and 80 percent of men cannot read and write. These are also the people who are the decision makers of a society anywhere. If they cannot read and write, what kind of decisions can they make? If they cannot read, they cannot sign their name to a deed. If they cannot read the tax form from the government, what kind of society can they build? So, over the next twenty years, it is these adults, not the kids in school, that are the decision makers of Afghanistan. I must pay attention to them; and I find it very meaningful.[69]

Since 2002, I have had a program of literacy, but I have it with a twist. The condition to coming to my class is that both husband and wife come jointly. It is a couple's literacy class.[70]

The results of the literacy classes are extremely apparent. Ten couples attend one class for twelve months. The changes that occur in each individual are phenomenal, Gross says. Susan Andersen, a social psychology professor at New York University, has produced a video of couples she interviewed, called *Love Letters from Kabul*.[71]

Gross says her work with husbands and wives is very important.

When you bring them together, and both of them do not know the letter "A" ... they realize that both of them do not know this, and they start learning together. It is an extremely beautiful synergy that is created between husband and wife. Their relationship affects family life, it affects their community. Now that they can read and write, they become revered by their community. Other people bring their children to these people to read to them. They can read the name of their candidate. They can sign their own name. It's extremely meaningful for me. The need is very, very big.[72]

The Roqia Center also addresses education for women in leadership. The Center publishes educational material such as the book *Women in the Koran*, compiled of all the verses in the Qur'an that mention the words "woman" or "women," or applicable pronouns. The words were scattered throughout the 6,666 verses, which makes it difficult for people to really know what the Qur'an says regarding women, says Gross. She distributed this book at the Constitutional Loya Jirga, libraries, to scholars and women's advocates.[73]

The center's work with leaders is important because there were no women leaders under the Taliban and Gross doesn't want Afghanistan to be in that position again. Second, women leaders are necessitated by the absolute need of the modern world.[74]

The limitations of her adult education program are funding, convincing adults of the importance of the center's work, language (such as finding words they will understand for the concepts of democracy), and the culture of war, Gross says. Gaining trust of people is important. But in general, Gross finds her work rewarding and needed, and Afghans are enthusiastic about learning. Turnouts for the center's conferences are high. She concludes, "The support for Afghan women, the success of Afghan women, must remain on the world agenda."[75]

Employment

Traditionally, Afghan society has included women in public activities. In the early twentieth century, women received the right to vote. Women were teachers and politicians. In the Soviet invasion years, women were warriors during the Afghan resistance (1979–89). So, it was a cruel aberration when the Taliban upset this social order.[76]

The aberration was greatly modified by 2008. Haron Amin observes about Afghan women, "there are educators, there are government employees, there are teachers, there are professors, judges, lawyers, business people that are becoming active members of society."[77] He elaborates,

> Some don't know that well, others do, in the context qualifications for scholarships. In Japan right now, for example, a great ... number of the students seeking a bachelors degree, masters degree and PhD are women.... Under the National Action Plan for women of Afghanistan, [this] is going to be a monumental step in the context of improving conditions of women across Afghanistan. It's going to move along with the [Millennium Development Goals]. The aim is to significantly increase the number of female participation in all of the government institutions, including elected and appointed bodies in civil service.... Also, different departments have been created in various agencies in the government to improve women for further integration and also pay raise.[78]

Amin continues,

> Pay has not been an issue. What I can tell you specifically is that when I was in Kabul, I was in so many different offices. What I noticed is that people in Afghanistan don't have a problem with the whole pay scale the way people have in other parts of so many countries that I have seen. Afghanistan is very understandable because of the fact that they realize that if they're paid better, that means that the house will [become] a little bit better. So, a husband, for example, realizes that if he's working on a specific office, if he takes more money home, that means he can live better, his wife lives better, and his children live better. By the same token, if he has a colleague who is a female and this female takes the same amount of money home, he recognizes that she will live better, the husband will live better, and the children will live better. There's a sense of solidarity that exists among Afghans I have not seen in a lot of countries. In other places, it's much more an issue of sexist games. In Afghanistan it's much more a sense of community, a sense of helping one another out.[79]

In spite of the poverty, Amin believes that the people are living better than before. Progress exists across Afghanistan. He says,

> I see specific signs in Kabul. I see specific signs in the countryside. For example, a person unemployed in the countryside and a person unemployed in the city, both live in a very disadvantageous situation. But ... there is employment opportunity.... [In] Kabul, hundreds of thousands of people from Pakistan and other areas have come to work on the construction crews. A lot of the work Afghans do not want to do because they think it is beneath their dignity.... I was really shocked to think, okay how is [it] that we are hiring so many people from a foreign country and Afghans want to do [only] specific fields? So, yes, sometimes you look at specific things and there is no specific census, numbers or index or logic that explains why a person is a specific way, but it is that way. But from what I saw in Kabul, the impression is that it is having impact. For example, over three billion dollars in the 2006–2007 fiscal year came back from Afghan expats living overseas and bringing that money back to Afghanistan.[80]

Amin says the face of Afghanistan is changing. These changes reflect development that in turn results in a better standard of living, in part from employment opportunity. Amin provides examples.

> When one would go from Kabul to Charikar before the war there was only one gas station. Now you go between these two distances of some 60 or 70 kilometers, there are at least twenty gas stations. In Kabul,

traffic jams were unheard of. The city was barely handling 500,000 people. Now more than four million are living in Kabul. And more are being attracted to Kabul. Townships are popping up all over Kabul.... Twenty-four hundred buildings thus far inspected by the new mayor in the last six months have been told that they have not observed codes of construction and that some of them have been illegally built. Eighty percent of Kabul is not recognizable in the context of how much development has taken place. The Kabul of 2002 cannot be recognized. There has been so much development. Traffic jams. You go to the Logar, you see so much development. Yes, poverty still grounds us, but here's a fact. A person who [had] no hope to live is now living. A person who was living on bread is now having bread and soup. A person who was living on bread and soup is now having palau [Afghan rice], having meat and vegetables.[81]

The Challenges of Economic Vulnerability

Although positive things are happening for the people of Afghanistan, poverty remains a reality for many. Nasrine Abou-Bakre Gross says that for the ordinary women in Afghanistan,

> life is very difficult. Aside from unimagined poverty, daily life is extremely difficult, because Afghanistan does not have the things we take for granted in America. There is no electricity. There is no running water. There is no hot water. Fuel is extremely expensive and time-consuming to get.[82]

These items are necessities, not conveniences, says Gross. She describes conditions in her home in Afghanistan:

> I have to rely on a generator to have some electricity and I cannot have it all the time; and I cannot have a lot of electricity. I don't have a refrigerator. I have to cook for the meal of that moment, whether it's breakfast, lunch or dinner. In summer, it is so hot that you cannot keep lunch foods for dinner because it will spoil. Because they don't use preservatives for vegetables and fruit, if you buy those items from the market, they don't last even 24 hours. What you buy are not cleaned, so, for example, cooking spinach is something like a six hour job. It takes two to three hours to first clean the spinach.[83]

Gross says that this situation is just the tip of the iceberg for Afghan women, "Very few women can afford servants," she says. "All women have to do the cooking. Over 50 percent have to make the dough, bake their own bread in the home oven every day." Further:

> There is no drinking water. Many, many people don't have a well. The government has very few water networks. Women have to bring water from streams or from public wells and public pumps. Under those circumstances, washing clothes becomes a major chore. Then drying them. There is this dust in Afghanistan and dust gets everywhere. So, cleaning the house, cleaning the yard, dusting has to be done once or twice a day.[84]

Gross adds that if Afghan women work outside the home, they have to be at least twice as organized. Her work will require different kinds of clothing, and "she will find that readymade clothes are not available in Afghanistan. She will either have to sew them herself or go to a tailor. Most women make theirs and their children's clothing.[85]

Gross says that life is very hard and that she spends most of her own time just on daily chores and such questions as who will bring bread for her, who is going to cook, where will she get the gasoline, is the generator working, does the well have enough water, and who will dust the room? Chores, once completed, leave Gross with 20–30 percent of her day to devote to her purpose in Afghanistan, activism.[86]

In 2008, UNICEF reported that over 30 percent of Afghan children work and about 43 percent marry before they are eighteen years old.[87] The Afghanistan Independent Human Rights Commission found that economic vulnerability affected standard of living, child labor and child marriage. Regarding child labor, the commission specifically found that "the more economically vulnerable the household is, the higher the proportion of children [under age of 15] that are exposed to hazardous forms of work."[88] The work also prevented children from attending school. Over a third (37 percent) reported that at least one child in the family works and among them 31 percent stated that their children were the only source of family income. Hazardous work includes carrying heavy loads (27.9 percent) and working under excessive heat, cold, or noise (15.3 percent).[89]

Regarding child marriage and economic vulnerability, the commission found that "the more economically vulnerable a household is, the higher the proportion of children who marry underage (before the age of sixteen). The majority (54.6 percent) of those interviewees who said their children married before the age of sixteen explained that marriages were arranged to address/solve economic problems."[90] Lack of employment was the main source of concern and a key obstacle to reintegration. Forty-five percent of returnees said it was the main cause of dissatisfaction and 17.6 percent of returnees indicated it as the main reason for leaving their places of origin. Lack of employment also was a cause of protracted displacement for 21.5 percent of internally displaced persons.[91]

Women and Work

Women's Roles in Work

Eighty percent of Afghans are employed in agriculture and related occupations and trades. These occupations have traditionally accounted for at least half the economy. War, displacement, constant droughts, flooding, the laying of mines, and the prolonged absence of natural resource management has led to massive effects on the environment and the depletion of resources. Rural unemployment is extremely high, over 50 percent. Large scale deportations of economic migrants from Iran and the return of refugees exacerbate unemployment. Oxfam recommends that any strategy to guarantee local-level support must ensure that rural women benefit, whether in farming or off-farm rural trades, and that their particular skills and resource needs are addressed.[92]

Women play a very important part in agricultural production, representing 30 percent of agricultural workers.[93] Depending on the region, women may spend as much time in work as their male counterpart or because of tradition, women may spend most or all of their time in household activities. In production employment, for example, opium, livestock and dairy products, most of women's labor is without pay, but their contribution is high. Only in the urban-based formal sector is women's participation high, for example, in teaching and in health professions.[94]

The traditional role is to constrain women's participation. That is, wage labor for women is viewed as the last resort and if they are paid, it is at half the rate or less than that paid to men. However, with the high fertility rate of 6.3 and maternal mortality rate of 1,600 per 100,000 live births, reproduction and health issues fill most of women's time. That production is needed for subsistence and services are sometimes absent also affect the female labor market. Other limitations include lack of ownership or control, and bypassing their legal right to inheritance and of capital. Thus, although the constitution guarantees women equal opportunity, in reality many are limited by familial control, where the male is expected to protect and provide for the women, per Islam, just as she is expected to bear the family honor.[95]

Gross maintains, "On a couple of occasions that President Karzai has publicly talked about women, the effect has been tremendous. This lack of social legitimacy for women and for modernity is one of the most important reasons that is keeping us confused and preventing us Afghans from moving forward — men and women, urban and rural, tribal and nontribal alike."[96] Gross elaborates that government should enforce the philosophy that official responsibility is as important as social obligations and that traditions should be defined so that they can be modified.

Unemployment and Women's Responses

Because Afghanistan is dealing with massive unemployment and poverty, many women go to work out of desperate need. Carlotta Gall lived with Afghan nomads and reports on the experiences of three women in 2003, one of whom, Nafisa Sahar, did "the most daring work," acting. Nafisa received a threat through an anonymous letter warning her to stay home, but she was not deterred. In fact, through her plays and sketches she encouraged Afghan women to get out and work and make their own decisions. Another woman, Jamila Raufi, a nurse, abandoned her burqa for a simple veil. Within blocks of her home a man in a taxi threw snuff in her face which stung her eyes and nose.[97]

The BBC met with villagers of Asad Khyl north of Kabul in September 2005 to find out how life had changed since 2005. The BBC reporter took questions submitted by readers. One question asked, in part: "Are there more opportunities for women to work and support themselves?"[98] A widow, Lal Bibi, answered that women stay at home because of lack of opportunity to work. Men can go to the bazaar and find work. She would like the government or the NGOs to establish tailoring, embroidery and

A few determined Afghan women are making the most of whatever economic opportunities are open to them — mostly in home-related spheres such as craft making. Ziba, a 20-year-old former refugee who returned from Pakistan, is one such entrepreneur, who has overcome numerous obstacles to establish a successful small business, her beauty salon named Golh Bahar. Ziba puts on makeup every morning before starting her work. Kabul, September 30, 2004 (AFP Photo).

literacy courses because then she could earn a living. In 2006, Lal Bibi took a course on how to keep cows and livestock. She borrowed money and bought a cow. She collects fodder for the cow from the gardens; then she sells the milk in the market to buy sugar, tea and basic food. She laments, "That is not enough for me. Everything is expensive.... Life is too difficult for me."[99]

Two women at sewing machines, August 15, 2004 (Ben Barber/USAID).

Still, women rank high percentagewise in fields such as health care and the media and are increasing their numbers in employment in fields such as the justice sector. (See Table 4.2 on the following page.) Haron Amin notes:

> More than ten TV stations have all female anchors, female producers. Some of them are twenty-four-hour stations. They're impacting lives. Close to 50 percent of the population already have TV. A lot of times if the husbands or the families in Afghanistan are forced to have TV, it's not because of the husbands, but because of the wives and because of the children. And by virtue of possessing these TVs, I think they are educating themselves. They're learning programs; they're learning about ... worldly matters, etc. More than 100 media stations have been established and more than 200 newspapers and magazines are sanctioned.[100]

In 2006, Afghan women judges took training in the United States. The judges reported, "Often drug running is the only work available in Afghanistan.... If employment opportunities improve and people learn more about the law, the situation would be better."[101] The judges explained

Table 4.2
Women's Participation in Employment and Limitations of the Education Sector

Sector

Labor Force

— 30% of agricultural workers are women
— Women receive three times less wages than men
— 50,000 war widows in Kabul, supporting an average of six dependents
— 38.2% of women are economically active
— In 2004, the per capita Gross Domestic Product was U.S. $402 for women as compared to U.S. $1,182 for men

Justice Sector

— 62 women or 4.2% out of 1547 sitting judges
— 35 women or 6.4% out of 546 prosecutors,
— 76 women or 6.1% out of 1241 attorneys
— No women in the Supreme Court Council
— Women head the family and juvenile courts

Note: An Afghan Women Judges Association was created in 2003, and there is also an Afghan Women Lawyers and Professionals Association

Security Services

— Less than 1% of police or military personnel are women
— 233 women police out of the total 62,407 as of February 2007
— 259 women or 0.6% of approximately 43,000 military personnel in the Afghan National Army
— No women in the auxiliary police force

Peace Building and Reconstruction

— 21,239 women or 24% compared to 67,212 (76%) men in the 9,394 Community Development Councils established by May 2007

Health

Note: A new Department of Women and Reproductive Health was established within the Ministry of Health in 2003. A Basic Package of Health Services has been developed which includes emergency obstetric care.

— 49.3% of 15,001 health care workers are women

Press/Media Sector

— 208 or 23.6% women out of the 881 staff members in the government press sector as of April 2007
— 20.9% were women staff members of one private daily newspaper in Kabul
— 202 women out of 1,950 staff members in private television in Kabul
— Most women work as cleaners and cooks in the media sector

Education

— 58.8% of students enrolling in teacher training institutions were women in 2005.

Limitations

— 15.8% estimated literacy rate for women compared to 31% for men
— 19% of schools are designated as girls schools
— 29% of educational districts have no designated girls schools
— 28.4% of the teachers were women in 2005
— one girl student for every two boys at primary level
— one girl for every three to four boys at secondary level
— 4.7% per annum decrease in the number of girls in secondary school during 2004–05

Source: "Situation of Women in Afghanistan, Fact Sheet 2008." United Nations Development Fund for Women (UNIFEM), http://Afghanistan.unifem.org/media/pubs/08/factsheet.html #labor (accessed August 17, 2008).

that the people who are apprehended are really victims of a larger problem. The druglords are not the ones who get caught. The ones who get caught become victims because they don't know the consequences of drug running and they don't know for whom they work.

The realized hope of employment lies in the greater hope of education for the children of Afghanistan. One field of opportunity lies in the explosion of job opportunities for skilled computer operators, especially in the urban areas. According to Help the Afghan Children, the majority of these jobs are being filled by non–Afghans. They believe an opportunity to address the swelling unemployment levels is being lost. Because of the destruction resulting from war, computer skills are rapidly becoming an important but missing element of education. The inability to gain practical computer skills affects girls by perpetuating forced marriages, early child-bearing, and the inability for young women to utilize their potential and lead productive lives.[102]

Each school Help the Afghan Children supports is equipped with a computer laboratory, computer workbooks, and a well-qualified instructor. Help the Afghan Children has been very successful and serves as an example of education's advantage for meaningful employment.

5

Health

When a woman dies in childbirth in Afghanistan, the entire family suffers because of her death.[1]
— Dr. Lynn Amowitz, senior medical researcher,
Physicians for Human Rights

Hope in the Health of Infants and Children

President Hamid Karzai explains progress in health care for children this way: nearly 90,000 children who would have died before their fifth birthday during Taliban rule would stay alive in 2007 because of improved healthcare. The child mortality rate for children under five had declined from 257 deaths per 1,000 live births in 2001 to 191 in 2006.[2]

Martin Bell's report for UNICEF, *Child Alert Afghanistan*, notes significant progress in the majority of the population. A greater number of people now has access to a basic package of health services that includes routine immunization. The percentage of children who received Vitamin A supplements rose from 56 in 2001 to 90 in 2006 and 95 in 2007. The UNICEF-supported polio eradication campaign resulted in a drop from thirty-one cases in 2006 to eleven in 2007 as of October.[3]

In January 2008, UNICEF announced that post–Taliban Afghanistan has made significant progress in reducing its under-age-five child mortality by 25 percent from 2001 through 2007. UNICEF attributed the improvement in the health sector and the reduction in child mortality to the political will of the Afghan government to improve health service, water supply and education.[4] UNICEF's *Humanitarian Action Report 2008* states that 23 percent of the total population has access to safe drinking water.[5]

The Afghanistan Independent Human Rights Commission reported that access to water was the second most critical issue presented by interviewees. Approximately half (52.2 percent) experienced lack of access to safe drinking water. Problems with water related to quality (47.5 percent), availability (24.1 percent), and physical accessibility (23.1 percent). The standard set by the World Health Organization holds water accessible if sources are available within a maximum of fifteen minutes walking distance from each household. About 36 percent of the interviewees reported having to walk for more than fifteen minutes one way to get water; among them, 35.1 percent have to walk more than one hour.[6]

UNICEF also cautioned that Afghanistan has a long way to go, in that the country is second in maternity mortality and third in child mortality in the world.[7] Preventable diseases such as pneumonia, poor nutrition, and diarrhea cause approximately 600 children under five to die every day. One out of four Afghan children does not reach a fifth birthday. In addition, only 28 percent of children with pneumonia reach an appropriate health-care provider, and only 48 percent of children with diarrhea receive "oral rehydration and continued feeding therapy."[8]

Just 14 percent of pregnant women have a skilled attendant during child delivery. More than half of children six to nine months old do not have proper breast feeding and complementary food. The result is that 39 percent of children under five are underweight, and the growth of 54 percent is stunted or improper.[9]

Access to Facilities

In 2005, the *Country Cooperation Strategy* report found that Afghanistan had 16 regional hospitals, 31 provincial hospitals, 70 district hospitals, 402 comprehensive health centers and 593 basic health centers. In 2003, a national hospital assessment revealed that in emergency obstetric care services, equipment, and human resources, Afghanistan had a total of 857 beds, served a monthly average of 22,652 patients, and delivered a monthly average of 7,961 babies (428 via caesarean sections). The country had twenty-seven obstetric operating tables, thirty-nine surgical lights, twenty caesarean section kits, and 365 gynecologists.[10]

The Afghanistan Independent Human Rights Commission reported in 2007 that primary health care facilities, either governmental (85.9 percent) or private (60.6 percent), were available for the majority. But the commission also found that significantly over one-third of all interviewees (36.9 percent) who had access to governmental health care facilities and 21.8 percent who had access to privately operated ones, do not use facilities, primarily because of the lack of physical accessibility. The second main reason that prevented people from getting needed health care was the poor quality of facilities — 21.8 percent cited this for governmental services and 31.9 percent for private facilities.[11]

Although the World Health Organization reported a decrease in the number of most types of health care personnel from 2001 to 2004, Ambassador Amin reports an increase from this very low base in 2007. The WHO reported in 2005, services have been extended to 77 percent of the population. The report concludes, "the majority of the Afghan population does not have access to a health facility and thus to the basic services."[12]

Habibullah, a patient at Kabul's main trauma center, Wazir Akbar Khan Provincial Hospital, January 24, 2006 (Ben Barber/USAID).

Table 5.1
Health Care Personnel Availability and Creation
per 100,000 population, 1999–2004

Personnel	1999	2001	2003	2004
Physicians	—	19	11	13.0
Dentists	—	3	—	1.5
Pharmacists	2.5	—	—	2.0
Nurses/Midwives	—	22	—	15.0
Paramedical Staff*	—	—	—	11.0
Community Health Workers	—	—	—	18.4
Others**	—	—	—	29.0

*vaccinators, sanitarians, radiology technicians, and lab technicians
**administrative technicians, support staff

Note: Due to a big difference between the salary scale of government and NGOs, the level of staff turnover has been escalated and has become a great concern.

Source: Ministry Public Health, 2004, 2005, Health Systems Profile, Country: Afghanistan, May 14, 2005, World Health Organization, Eastern Mediterranean Regional Office, Division of Health System and Services Development, Health Policy and Planning Unit, Table 7–1, 32. http://www.emro.who.int/afghanistan/Media/PDF/HealthSystemProfile-2005.pdf (accessed January 13, 2008).

Table 5.2
Human Resource Training Institutions for Health, 2004

Institution	Number	Capacity
Medical Schools	8	800
Postgraduate Training Institutions	—	—
Schools of Dentistry	1	30
Schools of Pharmacy	1	100
Nursing Schools	8	600
Midwifery Schools	8	150
Paramedical Training Institutes	4	400
Schools of Public Health	—	—

Note: Capacity is the annual number of graduates from these institutions.

Sources: Ministry of Public Health, 2004. Health Systems Profile, Country: Afghanistan, May 14, 2005, World Health Organization, Eastern Mediterranean Regional Office, Division of Health System and Services Development, Health Policy and Planning Unit, Table 7–2, 32–33, http://www.emro.who.int/afghanistan/Media/PDF/HealthSystemProfile-2005.pdf (accessed January 13, 2008).

With technical assistance from Johns Hopkins University and the Indian Institute of Health Management Research, the Afghan Ministry of Public Health evaluated Afghanistan's "Basic Package of Health Services" in 2006. A comparison of 2006 with the 2005 and 2004 scores shows a great deal of progress in the first two years of implementation of the Basic Package. Twenty-five out of 29 indicators improved. The report recognizes some need for improvement, saying that "in spite of these improvements, scores have decreased between 2004 and 2006 in several important areas — these include time spent with patients, facility infrastructure, presence of user-fee guidelines and the equity of patient satisfaction between the poor and the non-poor."[13]

The Ministry of Public Health reported that during the year 2006 the coverage of the Basic Package of Health Services increased from 77 to 82 percent of the population; the number of health facilities providing the package increased from 846 to 979; the number of active community health workers increased from 12,000 to 15,000 (half are female); the number of health facilities providing comprehensive emergency obstetric care increased from 79 to 89; staff have increased by 786; and 9,000 health care workers have been trained, of which half of the nurses are female.[14] In 2008, the ministry reported that the coverage of the Basic Package has increased from 9 percent in 2002 to above 80 percent in 2007. In addition, 70 percent of health facilities have at least one female staff member, compared to 45 percent in 2001. Nineteen community midwifery training centers in nineteen provinces have trained hundreds of community midwives.[15]

Maternal health care has also improved. Almost 2,400 midwives were trained and graduated from midwifery schools; over 70 percent of health facilities have at least one professional female health worker; use of prenatal care increased from 4.6 percent in 2003 to over 30 percent in 2006; and use of skilled birth attendants increased from 6 to 19 percent.[16]

In 2006, 233 health facilities were renovated or constructed. Basic services to hospitals were increased. Immunization of children and coverage of basic health services for children also increased. Twenty-six therapeutic feeding units were established. Over 2.1 million children under the age of five were screened for malnutrition during the first nine months of 2006. Work in tuberculosis detection and control of disease such as malaria has improved. But HIV/AIDS is described as a "looming threat," due to the "increase in number of injecting drug users and high number of HIV cases in neighboring countries."[17]

The government's development of its "Basic Package of Health Services" has helped assist women in their health care. In late 2007, Ambassador Amin expanded on other areas of progress in the health field that can aid increase in services:

> Thousands of females are being trained as nurses. Infant mortality has been cut by 25 percent. Midwives are being trained throughout the country. More than 83 percent of the population has access to basic health care packages, compared to less than 20 percent five years ago. Health care is booming in Afghanistan, including not only just for needs, but we are now talking about cosmetic surgery in Herat; we are looking at cosmetic surgery in Kabul; we are looking at breast cancer clinics in Mazaar and Kabul. So, these are the things that are happening across Afghanistan. We actually began from a very low base. We ... had maybe a hundred people that had any expertise in the health sector and now we've got thousands. And ... a great deal of focus is on the issue of infant mortality, on the issue of women's health ... and access to proper facilities.[18]

Midwives train to save lives, Faizabad, Badakshan Province, Afghanistan, January 24, 2006 (Ben Barber/USAID).

Future doctors. Students chat outside Kabul Medical University, which is being fixed up with U.S. and other international aid, 2006 (Ben Barber/ USAID).

But many Afghan people are caught in crossfire and out of reach of humanitarian assistance as a result of decades of war. Along with unabated attacks on schools and violence, a decaying and under-resourced health system affects Afghans. Bell adds that, although significant progress has been made in education and health care, "far too many children in Afghanistan are missing out" in these areas.[19] Life expectancy for the total population is estimated at 43.77 years; for males, 43.6 years; and for females, 43.96 years (2007 estimate).[20]

Food Insecurity

The Afghanistan Independent Human Rights Commission reported in 2007 that their findings confirmed an alarming level of chronic or transient food shortages. Only 37.7 percent of interviewees said that their household had a stable income source, and 60.3 percent earned less than 50 Afghanis (one U.S. dollar) per day.[21] The majority of interviewees live in absolute poverty as defined by World Bank, they said.

The Oxfam report points out that 48 percent of children, or about six million, are stunted due to malnourishment, which affects health and performance in school. Universal midday meals would alleviate hunger as well as affect enrollment, high drop-out rates and overall performance. Although targeted food programs provide incentives to retain children in school, they do not meet the scale of malnutrition. In addition, they are not cost effective and identification of those in need is difficult.[22] Also to be considered is that the widespread nutritional deficiency associated with food insecurity is at times made worse by drought conditions.[23]

The UNICEF *Humanitarian Action Report for 2008* indicates Afghanistan's maternal mortality ratio remains high at 1,600 deaths per 100,000 live births and the infant mortality rate is 165 per 1,000 live births. One child out of every four does not survive his or her fifth birthday. Reasons for the high infant mortality is repeated drought, chronic household food shortage, widespread inappropriate feeding and caring practices. Seven percent of children under five suffer from acute malnutrition and 54 percent are chronically malnourished. Immunization coverage for DPT1, DPT3 and measles is estimated at 90, 77 and 68 percent respectively. Health services are available in 82 percent of districts, but there is a significant population without access to such services.[24]

For children, diarrhea, acute respiratory infections, and vaccine-preventable illnesses account for 60 percent of deaths. Among adults, tuberculosis causes an estimated 15,000 deaths per year, with women accounting for 70 percent of detected cases. Almost half of all deaths among women of reproductive age are a result of pregnancy and childbirth. More than three-fourths of these deaths are preventable.[25] Mohammad Amin Fatimi, health minister, estimates that 250,000 children under five die every year from malnutrition, diarrhea, TB and malaria. The youngest children make up the majority of the high child mortality rate. He said, "Many newborns are dying because they don't have access to immediate healthcare."[26]

Maternal Health

The UNICEF *Child Alert* report also argues strongly for the "woeful" maternal mortality rate to be addressed.[27] The World Bank similarly reports that child health and women's reproductive health indicators in Afghanistan are among the most unfavorable in the world. The alarming conditions of women are not the result of deliberate gender discrimination in households, but of poverty, lack of health facilities and certain social factors such as low marriage age and high fertility. Childbirth is too frequent and women have too many children. Another cause is the widespread reluctance to let women seek medical assistance from male health workers, lack of awareness of maternal health care among men and women, and insufficient awareness of health, hygiene and nutrition.[28] Women are treated by male physicians. The U.S. Agency for International Development has photographed a case of a male doctor treating a child because the mother can now leave home. The *Country Cooperation Strategy for WHO and Islamic Republic of Afghanistan 2005 to 2009* states, "Among all other determinants of ill-health, income poverty has the strongest impact on health outcomes.[29]

The World Bank reports that in 2002 women's health indicators in Afghanistan were a children-under-five mortality rate of 257 per 1,000, infant mortality rate of 165 per 1,000, and an estimated maternal mortality rate of 16 per 1,000 live births; a rate of chronic malnutrition (moder-

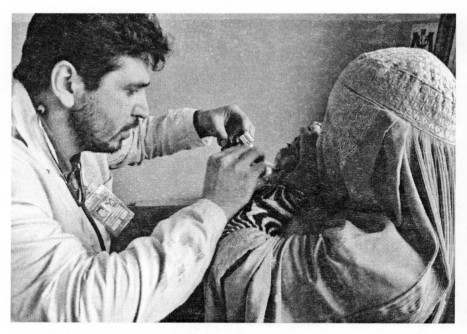

A male doctor is now allowed to treat a child that is being held by its mother since there are no longer any Taliban limits on women leaving the home and having contact with men outside their family. March 18, 2003 (M. Lueders/ USAID).

ate or severe stunting) of approximately 50 percent; and very high rates of disability due to polio, cerebral palsy and conflict (including land mines).[30]

The UN Development Fund for Woman's 2007 indicators for maternal mortality were similar, 1,600 to 1,900 deaths per 100,000 live births, the second highest maternal mortality rate in the world.[31] *Country Cooperation Strategy* estimates that 25,000 women die every year of pregnancy-related complications.[32] This high figure is certainly understandable depending on whether a woman has professional care or whether she can access care. With time, these figures may decline because in 2003, a Department of Women and Reproductive Health was established within the Ministry of Health, and the Basic Package of Health Services includes emergency obstetric care.[33]

Table 5.3
Limitations on Women's Health, 2007

Limitations

— One woman dies every 29 minutes in childbirth (1,600 to 1,900 deaths per 100,000 live births, the second highest maternal mortality rate in the world)
—14% of births have skilled attendants present, and 12% of women receive professional antenatal care
— 30% to 90% of women, depending on location, in rural areas cannot access health care
— Average woman had 7.4 children in 2004
— Average life expectancy for women in Afghanistan is 44 years
—16,000 women die out of 25,000 Afghans who die from tuberculosis each year
— 48% of women are iron-deficient

Note: A new Department of Women and Reproductive Health was established within the Ministry of Health in 2003. A Basic Package of Health Services has been developed which includes emergency obstetric care.

Source: "Situation of Women in Afghanistan, Fact Sheet 2008." United Nations Development Fund for Women (UNIFEM), http://Afghanistan.unifem.org/media/pubs/08/factsheet.html (accessed August 20, 2008).

Context for Low Health Indicators

UNICEF indicates that after the fall of the Taliban 1,600 women died for every 100,000 live births. But many women were and still are dying during and after pregnancy due to poverty, traditional cultural practices, difficult terrain and an acute shortage of female medical professionals. The shortage of female health workers is especially crucial because family tradition dictates that it is unacceptable for a woman to be treated by a man unless her situation is critical.[34]

The World Health Organization 2005 *Health Systems Profile—Afghanistan* reported, "Within the health sector, the most important constraint to improving health status is lack of access to basic health services in much of the country."[35] This constraint is illustrated through the June 2007 interviews of Horia Mossadeq, a human rights and women's rights activist, which highlight the relationship of lack of access to services to infant and maternal death. In one case, a 25-year-old woman lived in a remote part of the country in the northeastern province of Badakshan. She traveled two hours in excruciating pain to the nearest hospital, in Faizabad. The doctors saved the mother's life, but it was too late for the baby, who died. The mother would have died, too, had she not gotten help in time. Mossadeq points out that whatever the mortality rates indicate, "they still speak of huge gaps in health care for women, more than five years after Afghanistan emerged from the years of conflict."[36] She adds that few roads access Badakshan and that the donkey is most often the transportation available. Most women give birth at home and qualified help rarely is available. Many parts of Badakshan are unreachable in winter, six to seven months of the year. In combination with these transportation issues, less visible is rising drug abuse. Many people who live far from clinics turn to opium as medicine.

Mossadeq relates the story of a man, Sync Mohamaddin, who had to care for his five children after his fifty-five-year-old wife died after hemorrhaging badly after giving birth to their sixth child, at home. At the neighbors' urging, he waited before taking her to the medical center and she bled to death. He had to give the baby away because he couldn't take care of it. The remaining children did not have enough to eat because he could not leave them to work in the flour mill. Mossadeq believes his wife would have benefited from advice at a family planning clinic in Badakshan's main hospital. The UNICEF study found that 97 percent of women questioned were not using any form of contraceptive. Although the average fertility rate is seven children, many women will have up to ten or thirteen pregnancies.[37]

Prevention of Maternal Deaths

"One in seven women will die from pregnancy and childbirth in Afghanistan,"[38] writes Douglas Huber, M.D. He adds that the quickest, easiest, and most inexpensive method to prevent maternal deaths is with contraception. Huber's main message is that women should strive to have three-year birth intervals. This is supported by the Qur'an: "And mothers shall suckle their children two full years for those who wish to complete breast-feeding" Baqara (Sura 2:233).

Huber conducted a study that took place in three areas of Afghanistan: Tormai, Ghazni; Islam Qala, Herat; and Farza, Kabul Province. It reached important conclusions:

• Ethnic and cultural differences are not a barrier for contraception

• Community and religious leaders, when well informed, will support birth spacing and modern contraceptives

• Contraceptive method preferences vary widely, and leadership of mullahs may determine method mix.[39]

Familial support for contraception was found in a husband's story from Islam Qala. A senior imam in a Pashtoon area of Herat province spoke during a meeting with other mullahs:

> Yes, I know about family planning. In fact my wife has been using injectable contraceptives for six months. See, here in my notebook I keep the date for her next injection to help remind her, because she cannot read.[40]

The *woleswal* (mayor) of Farza, a Pashto-speaking area in rural Kabul Province, also spoke in favor of birth spacing:

> Eight months ago, talking about contraception was a taboo. Now people easily talk about birth-spacing practice and its importance. No matter where people get together, birth spacing has become a value within our people and they know it's the most effective and quick way to reduce maternal and child death.[41]

In addition to contraception matters, transportation issues and the use of opium for medicinal purposes, a reluctance to go to clinics exists. Sometimes women die because they are not permitted to go to the clinic, forbidden either by husband or relatives. The lack of permission and sometimes accompanying violence are coupled by the high illiteracy rate in some places where women are not cognizant of their rights. Sync Farzana grants that through parliament women have more voice today than they ever did, but she laments, "I'm not happy with all the change that happened in these five years. I was expecting more. But it doesn't mean that there is no change. But I want more."[42]

Sync Farzana's desire for more change illustrates very well one of the problems the Afghan government faces, that women want change faster then it can happen because they want to move forward.[43] According to Mossadeq, Farzana represents that desire to move forward because "like most Afghans [Farzana] has a deep hope that the next twenty-five years, even if they're difficult, will be nothing like the previous twenty-five....

It's a difficult birth, she says. But, as the mothers and midwives of Badakshan will tell her for nothing, there's no such thing as an easy birth in their country."[44]

Need for Basic Services

The World Health Organization maintains that if most of the Afghan population had access to the basic services, it could make a big difference to their health. For example, routine immunization coverage (DPT3) was estimated to be only 54 and 66 percent in 2003 and 2004 respectively. Female staff are lacking at 40 percent of existing health facilities, which means that women are not likely to access those facilities. More than 80 percent of existing services are provided by non-governmental organizations.[45] The WHO lists other factors limiting health care: shortage of skilled health staff in rural areas; lack of managerial capacity, particularly at the provincial level; and managerial and organizational structures that do not provide incentives or accountability for results. (See Tables 5.2 and 5.3.)

In 2006, the World Bank found that many elements helped to bring about the low health indicators, including the lack of access to basic health facilities. Only 9 percent of rural households surveyed in 2003 reported a health facility in their village. Even when facilities exist in rural areas, female staff is lacking. Infrastructure (roads and transportation) and security are deficient, which reduces mobility and access. The absence of clean drinking water and sanitation facilities contributes to a very high level of water-borne diseases.[46] The United States Agency for International Development says that there is one doctor per 6,000 people, and one nurse per 2,500 people.[47]

Unrelenting Damage from War

Land Mines

Afghanistan was one of the most heavily land-mined countries in the world, second only to Colombia. But almost 60 percent of the country

Women and children waiting at an Afghan medical clinic, March 17, 2003 (M. Lueders/USAID).

has been cleared, with all known stockpiles destroyed. An $80-million funding contribution from Canada will encourage a mine-free Afghanistan. This donation will help meet the chronic lack of resources to meet the needs of tens of thousands of land mine victims who will need health care and assistance the rest of their lives.[48]

Nawa District of Ghazni Province: A Most Dangerous Area

In December 2007, C. J. Chivers reported on several villages where children suffer. A bright spot existed in possibly the most dangerous place in the world, the Nawa District of Ghazni Province, an isolated region near Pakistan, where the Taliban operate with confidence and the Afghan government's presence is almost nonexistent. A ray of hope beamed through a company of paratroopers from the U.S. 82nd Airborne Division that patrolled the region throughout early December 2007. Chivers wrote, "Each patrol was a foray into villages regarded as Taliban sanctuaries."[49] The Taliban did not confront the heavily armed paratroopers. Once the villagers realized that medics were with the platoons, they brought their sick children for help. The medics found children with ailments such as burns, skin infections, distended scrapes, scorpion and spider bites, bleeding ears, dimmed eyes and severe coughs. Some children were bandaged in dirty rags. Others were wheeled in wheelbarrows because they were not strong enough to walk.

This very unsafe area, the Nawa District, is for the most part out of the reach of the Afghan government or the American military. Within the district is a transit route for insurgents who travel between Afghanistan and the tribal areas of Pakistan. A military captain says, "The Taliban has made it abundantly clear that no outside doctors, no outside medical help, can work in this district.... The government is trying to provide services, the message goes, while the Taliban tries to take services away. The government and the military plan to travel in the region soon with doctors and assess the problems and try to distribute aid and administer vaccinations."[50] Only one known physician, Dr. Nasibullah, exists in the district, and this doctor almost exclusively treats the Taliban's fighters.

Afghanistan as a Whole

Southern Afghanistan is a particularly dangerous area, but other parts are also unsafe. For example, in June 2004, the international humanitarian organization Doctors Without Borders/Médecins Sans Frontières closed all of its programs in Afghanistan. Five of the group's workers in a clearly marked vehicle were ambushed in the northwestern province of Badghis. The workers were shot. The attack was unprecedented in the years since 1980 when Doctors Without Borders began working in Afghanistan. The Taliban claimed the organization worked for American interests; its founding principle, however, is the separation of aid from political motives. The organization had in May 2004 publicly condemned the coalition forces distribution of leaflets in southern Afghanistan. The forces informed the public that providing information about the Taliban and al-Qa'ida was necessary to continue to receive aid. The government of Afghanistan did not arrest the offenders.[51]

Mental Health

Over two million Afghans suffer from levels of stress disorder due to the long period of conflict, according to the estimates in the *Country Cooperation Strategy* report. Affected is the capacity of the health care system to respond to the mental health needs. Mental health has not been addressed in the past decades and little is known about patterns of mental illness. In prewar time, studies indicate that Afghanistan's mental health was not that different from other developing countries. During the Taliban regime, high percentages of women living in the Taliban-controlled area compared with non–Taliban areas, suffered from major depression, 78 to 28 percent respectively; and from suicidal ideation, 65 to 18 percent respectively.[52] Another study found that 42 percent of women suffered post-traumatic stress, 97 percent experienced depression and 86 percent had anxiety.[53]

The high rates of mental problems may be related to Taliban policies of gender segregation and denial of basic human rights to women. Further the report states, "The fall of the Taliban regime, however, has not resulted in an improvement in the mental health status of the population."[54] A nationwide survey conducted in the first year after the U.S.-led invasion found high levels of depression symptoms (male: 59.1 percent, female: 73.4 percent), anxiety symptoms (male 59.3 percent, female 83.5 percent) and post-traumatic stress disorder (male 32.1 percent, female 48.3 percent). Those people with physical disabilities had a higher chance of developing mental problems. A 2004 CARE study reported that 78.6 percent of widows in Kabul had symptoms of depression.[55]

In 2004, a study supported by the U.S. Centers for Disease Control and Prevention confirmed the existence of widespread exposure to trauma and the great extent of mental health problems among Afghans in post-conflict Afghanistan. Afghans exhibited high degrees of symptoms of depression, anxiety, and PTSD. Women and disabled respondents had significantly poorer mental health than men and nondisabled respondents. Donors and health care planners need to address the lack of mental care resources, facilities, and trained mental health care professionals in Afghanistan.[56]

The Challenges

"The biggest obstacle to the post-conflict health system is the threat of renewed conflict," states the *Country Cooperation Strategy Report*.[57] In 2005, the report looked upon Afghanistan as a post-conflict state and evaluated the country as having been remarkably stable. It also predicted that with more female health workers, the usage of health facilities would improve. The report listed twenty-one points in its summary of some of the main health challenges confronting the health sector.

• Provide technical support in policy and management to meet the rapidly evolving health system

• Seek increase in national resources and less dependency on uncertain external funds

• Develop policies for health care financing based on people's ability and willingness to pay

• Strengthen government monitoring

• Increase access to health care

• Standardize health facilities

• Increase the role of the public sector in delivery of Basic Package of Health Services and Essential Package of Hospital Services in the medium to long term

• Develop a referral policy and implementation plans

• Increase the number of trained health staff, especially female mid-level health workers and midwives

• Increase the number of female health workers

• Monitor and evaluate the quality care now that health services are available to 70 percent of the population

• Increase the number of available traditional birth attendant health workers

• Increase managerial capacity and define responsibilities between all levels of the health care system

• Continue to relieve communicable diseases such as tuberculosis, malaria and vaccine-preventable diseases

• Increase the number of prenatal and postnatal care and trained midwives

• Decrease food insecurity to fight against malnutrition in general and in women and girls of child-bearing age and children under five

• Increase trained personnel in mental health

• Increase capacity of the government to manage natural and human-caused disasters

• Increase awareness among medical practitioners regarding medical ethics and the need to approach patients with compassion

• Construct a well-designed Information, Education and Communication plan and strategy for communicating health messages to all sections of the population, with special emphasis on the needs of young children, girls and women of childbearing age

• Assist in the efforts by other sectors for clean water supply and sanitation facilities disorders.

Government Goals

After the "Interim Health Strategy 2002 to 2004," the Ministry of Public Health formulated a National Health Policy for 2005 to 2009 and a National Health Strategy for 2005 to 2006. These outlined the course of actions the Ministry would take for the following five years. According to the *Country Cooperation Strategy* report, the overall goal of the health policy is

> to develop the health sector to improve the health of the people of Afghanistan, especially women and children, through implementing the basic package of health services and the essential package of hospital services as the standard, agreed-upon minimum of health care to be provided at each level of the health system.[58]

The National Health Policy Objective for this period is to reduce the high levels of mortality and morbidity by improving access to quality emergency and routine reproductive and child health services; increasing the coverage and quality of services to prevent and treat communicable diseases and malnutrition among children and adults; strengthening institutional development and management at central and provincial levels to ensure the effective and cost-efficient delivery of quality health services; and further developing the capacity of health personnel to manage and better deliver quality health services, including services for diagnosis and treatment of mental health disorders.[59]

Conclusion

In 2005, Dr. Sima Samar, chair of the Afghanistan Independent Human Rights Commission, said that security for women also means access to basic human rights such as health care, especially reproductive health care. In the last twenty-five years, women have been denied reproductive health care. Samar said,

> as a result, most women have eight to ten children. Most women have never seen a doctor before and are in very poor health from all of these pregnancies. They cannot feed all of these children, and, with these children, they cannot work or take part in political activities. Having reproductive health care really is a requirement for women to be empowered. We also need training and job opportunities for women, as well as for former war combatants so they can put down their guns and see there is a future without war and to reduce poverty.[60]

In 2008, progress is being made in providing health services in Afghanistan, but challenges remain, not the least of which is the negative effect of years of conflict. It is important to place numerical characterizations in that context. Differences in reports are mostly slight. Although women have specific reproductive health needs, we can readily see that both genders are in need of health services. As Amin states,

> If a person says that maternal mortality is so high in Afghanistan, well, by the same token, if there is no hospital, if a person has cancer, if a person has a wounded leg, or if a person has a very, very small prob-

lem such as diarrhea, all could be equally bound to death.... [It's not] just the women of Afghanistan that have not been taken care of.... Nobody gets help. For example, if we say that today women are not cared for enough in Afghanistan ... we [should not] deny the fact or ... simply overlook the fact [of] those [who] are handicapped in Afghanistan, the majority of people [who] have been in the war ... lost a leg ... lost a hand ... lost an eye or part of their body, and nobody cares about them.... [W]hen infrastructure is being put in place ... we have to understand ... that it is being done across the board, and [that] the lack of it means that a huge segment of society will be neglected.[61]

Although peace and security and justice for all is not yet fully attained in Afghanistan, hope appears in the words of the *Country Cooperation Strategy* report: "Every step taken toward reducing poverty and achieving broad-based economic growth can be a step toward conflict prevention."[62] And in doing so, more health care to a greater number of Afghans is more possible.

6

Voices and Images of Afghan People

by ROSEMARIE SKAINE *and*
LINA ABIRAFEH

The world thought they could bring freedom to Afghan women, [but] freedom is only won from the inside.

— Afghan man[1]

What have the changes in Afghanistan since 2001 meant to the Afghans' sense of identity and their relationships? Through images and text, and by listening to their voices, Dr. Lina Abirafeh and I recorded Afghan accounts of life in Afghanistan.

The voices of Afghan women, including the profile of General Aziza Nazari in Part I of this chapter, result from interviews conducted by Abirafeh as part of her research in Afghanistan between 2002 and 2006 on gendered interventions in the country. Her research, which was included in her doctoral dissertation at the Development Studies Institute at the London School of Economics and Political Science, addresses gender-focused international aid in Afghanistan in the aftermath of the external and civil conflicts and focuses on the period from the Bonn Agreement in December 2001 to September 2005.[2]

The profiles of Afghan leaders in Part II are written by Rosemarie Skaine.

Part I: Voices of Afghan Citizens

Couples and Family Members

In discussions with couples, the oft-repeated phrase, *inja Afghanistan ast*, meaning "this is Afghanistan," was used both by men and women frequently to punctuate a phrase. Women used it in exasperation to rationalize "bad things" that happened to them. Men used this line to justify the situation of women and as a counter to strong pushes for change and importing alien ideologies. "This is Afghanistan," I was told on many occasions. "Those things just don't work here." Both women and men conveyed a sense that because "this is Afghanistan," things were not going to change — and certainly not in the way that the aid apparatus expected. It was therefore important to compare not only women and men as separate entities but also women and men from the same household in order to determine how they define what Afghanistan is within their own households. These profiles of couples reveal the differing dynamics between men and women animating each household.[3]

Fatima and Amanullah, Wife and Husband[4]

Fatima is in her early thirties. She has had less than two years of education. Amanullah is forty-one years old and has had seven years of education. The couple is originally from rural Afghanistan but they moved to Kabul two years ago to live with Amanullah's brother in hopes of finding work and providing for their three children. Fatima explained that Amanullah's brother, her brother-in-law, is bitter about the extensive focus on women. He is not happy that Fatima attends training sessions, and tries to convince Amanullah to prevent her from going out. Many fights have broken out in the household as a result. Amanullah is beginning to think that participating in training is not such a good idea. Neither Fatima nor Amanullah are particularly pleased with the efforts of the aid institutions. Amanullah is concerned that Fatima will start to respect him less with all these new ideas she is gaining from the training program. Fatima complained: "You tell me what my rights are, but what is the point if he won't give them to me? He should understand them first!"

Zainab and Ahmadi, Wife and Husband[5]

Zainab and Ahmadi are from central Afghanistan. Their livelihood was based on agriculture. They are not happy to be in Kabul and find that they do not like the direction Afghanistan is moving in these new times. Zainab sees a lot of violence against women around her. She sees this as a new manifestation of an old struggle, but the difference today is that the "position of women is better than men in the society. Priority is given to women in every aspect of opportunities." Ahmadi is a day laborer and is able to bring home an irregular income. He is still hopeful that he will find more stable work. As long as he is working, he says that he is happy that Zainab is learning a new skill. He sees that other men are cruel and angry, and he does not think this will happen to him.

Sweeta and Payman, Wife and Husband[6]

Sweeta and Payman are in their thirties. She has had a few years of education. Payman has had nearly ten years of education and is a teacher by trade, although currently unemployed. Sweeta feels that Payman's profession as a teacher has helped her to have greater access to education and training. But she knows that Payman is unhappy that he is not working. The aid apparatus has done nothing for men, she says. "My husband says that they make men angry when they do nothing for them and only offer opportunities to women. He is a teacher so he understands how people think about these things." Sweeta feels that recent changes have brought "uproar to families." Payman agrees that he has seen an increase in family conflict because women are no longer satisfied "with what men expected from them."

Sara and Waheed, Daughter and Father[7]

Sara is eighteen years old. She is not in school, and this upsets her. She says that women in Afghanistan still cannot study and work, despite what they are told to believe. Her father appears to be an advocate of education for women and men, but he does not think the current climate is conducive for Sara to go to school. He explained that "since the Ameri-

125

cans came, we are told that men and women have freedom and can work outside and learn," but he feels that the situation is still unstable. Both Sara and Waheed feel that things were better for men and women before "the Americans came." Sara says that "some men think that women are being cared for more than men. But the reality is that both men and women suffer."

Women

The following are life stories from select women who were interviewed. These women all felt the need to talk about their lives and their contexts. Many women began the interviews with stories of their past as a way to illustrate their unhappiness in the present and the extent to which their lives have not improved. The profiles in 2005 provide a sample of the perceptions and experiences of women four years into Afghanistan's aftermath. There is more sadness that characterizes these stories, and noticeably less hope than interviews done in 2002. There is also a hint of disappointment in the lack of changes in their lives in the past three years. In fact, these women felt that their expectations were raised and now their hopes are further thwarted. Their stories speak to these themes.

Wahida[8]

I want to tell you about my tragic life. Twenty years ago, I was a young single girl. I studied in school and my only dream was to be educated and serve my country. But one day — I can still remember it — when I came home from school, I realized that my cruel parents had promised me to an army officer without letting me know. Nine days after my engagement I got married and I went to my in-law's family. I suffered a lot after that day. My marriage was terrible. Life was getting worse day by day. Then many years passed in my hard life. My husband developed mental problems because of the war. We tried to cure him, but he did not get well. One day he left us. It has been eleven years and I do not know if he is alive or dead. I have a son from my lost husband. I lived with my father-in-law but he was not kind to me and didn't support me. I went to live with my mother and we went to Pakistan where we spent two years as refugees. We heard about peace and the new regime, so we came back to our country. Now I am free to go outside the house and work. I want to make a good life for myself and my son. I want to make a small amount of money to save for my son's future. My story is very long. If I tell it all, days and nights will pass and I still won't be finished. So I will stop now in hope of peace in my country.

Homa[9]

I have five children. I am jobless and I don't work. My youngest child is in second grade at school. I don't know how to provide clothes and food for ourselves. It is very difficult for me. I raised my children with difficulty. I fed them with dry bread, because I didn't want people to tell me that I do not know how to look after my children. They are going to school, but I can't provide them school supplies and also clothes and shoes. I don't know from where I should provide them these things.

Bibi Shirine[10]

In our country according to the cultural system no father asks his daughter regarding her life. Without asking, my father gave me to a man and we got married. Fortunately I was happy with my husband a long time and God has given us four nice children. After a long time, when the conflict started in our country, I lost my husband and the difficulty has shown her face to me. No one helped us, my children and me. I sold my only home and spent it all for my children, feeding. There was no job for me and I started to sell my home assets to continue my life. Now I am old and I cannot work. We spent our life in very difficulties.

Mahboba[11]

My husband is disabled. I have six children but they are small and can't work. I and my daughter are working hard to earn money to provide a piece of bread for ourselves. I don't have any house. We have to live in a kitchen with my children. During the fightings, also, we lived here in this kitchen, because we couldn't afford to live anywhere else. I've spent

127

days in hunger, nights in the darkness without any light or electricity. I am not able to prepare anything for my family. We are in debt. I have more to tell you but you may become sad so I will bring my story to an end. Maybe you know about the life of an Afghan woman, filled with so much pain and difficulty that I'm not able to express it.

Maimona[12]

We have been immigrants in Pakistan in a tent three times. When I was five, my father died. And my mother died twelve years ago. I have one sister. My brother was martyred fifteen years ago in fighting. From the time we came back to our homeland from Pakistan we haven't had a house. I live in Khairkhana in a shop which is someone's property. I am washing clothes to earn money to provide my family expenses. My husband is not a good person; he always hits me and my children. I was an official worker in government during the Taliban regime. I was fired from my job. I was begging from shops and houses. I have worn burqa and cried and gone begging, and I have got a mental problem.

Hafiza[13]

I am living with twelve members of my family in a rental house. We don't have salary and we don't have jobs. We have many economic problems. And we are wondering how to continue our life. My husband is jobless. I have a baby that I can't support with my own milk because we are not eating good foods. There is no milk in my breasts.

One Woman's Life History Mariyam: Waiting for Change[14]

Mariyam was thirty-five years old. She was a mother of two small children. She could not read and hoped that one day she would have enough "free space in [her] head to think of such things." For the present she had to find a way to support her children, because her husband could not. Her family lived in one small room and shared a cooking space with a family in an adjacent room. "This is how our lives have become, in this time of peace," she said. Her husband was unemployed. He tried to find work as a day laborer but was not able to bring home a steady income. "He is angry," Mariyam explained, "and so he has turned on me, and turned to drugs. What can I do but tolerate this? I am a woman, after all."

Mariyam told the story of how her life had changed:

> My husband was kinder to me during the Taliban time. We were both scared. I felt safer then. We both had no opportunity for work or leaving the house. Life was very difficult but we struggled together. We were equal in our suffering.
>
> [Today] Afghan men are not given chances. But this is not our fault. Afghan women have always been patient, strong, brave, silent. We do what we must do to support our families and feed our children. If I don't go out and take advantage of this [waves hand around organization office], how will we live? He cannot. He wanted to before, but now he is an addict and he is useless to us. But he is my husband and I have no choice.

Mariyam felt that relations between men and women were deteriorating, not just in her household, but in those she saw around her: "Women are still struggling to make better their relations with men. It is not easy because there is still violence against them. It is a man's job to take care of the family and children financially. In most families that I have seen, relations have gotten worse because of poor economy. It is a bad thing, this change."

Mariyam explained that the tension between her and her husband was primarily because she had become the "man" in the family. Further, she was going out of the house. And, even more serious, she was "involved with foreigners." It was not just her husband, she explained. "Men don't like their women out of the house, especially with foreigners." She elaborated:

> I wish that women would work in local and governmental organizations and schools, not in foreign NGOs. It will cause them problems with the men if they work with foreigners. But I am here because this is where I get money.
>
> If there were opportunities for men to work, and for [Afghan] men and women to work together, things [would] change. But I do not know what opportunities men have. I see many of them without opportunities. Organizations are promising rights that women cannot achieve and cannot understand. On paper, women have been given rights and freedom. But in my mind, women expected more rights because that was what was promised to them.

Mariyam was not unlike other Afghan women she knew in that she was able to make astute observations about the work of the aid apparatus and the impact its presence and programs have had. She explained:

> Women are the center of interest for everyone. I never imagined I would see a day where foreign people don't stop talking about Afghan women. Every day in this organization some people come, some journalists come, and they want us to tell them that our lives are better. They want us to tell them that we are not wearing chaddari, that we are happy. They think we are stupid. And when they go away, we laugh because we have nothing else we can do. The world is watching, and this is what they want to see.

Mariyam had the following to say about the international obsession with the chaddari:

> The foreigners say, "remove your bourka, *bourka kharab* (bourka is bad)," but I say Afghanistan *kharab*. Afghan men *kharab*. Until we change this — and we will never change it — my chaddari protects me. I put it on and "where is Mariyam?" No one knows. And Mariyam comes and Mariyam goes. And Mariyam stays safe. What choice do I have?

Still, Mariyam was able to end on a positive note. "I hope for a bright future," she said. "What else can we do but hope?"

General Aziza Nazari: Making Change[15]

General Aziza Nazari was the deputy of the Human Rights Department in the Ministry of the Interior. She also represented the Afghanistan Independent Human Rights Commission in the ministry. She was tasked with training and assigning women police officers to handle women's security issues. General Nazari also worked to sensitize men in the ministry to women's human rights and security.

General Nazari's story was a rare one. She had served with the Afghan police for thirty-one years. In 2002, she became a general. Her father was in the military, and although he was a liberal man he did not want his daughter to follow suit. General Nazari recalled her father taking a trip to Turkey and returning with new ideas about women. He began to advocate for women's education, and he expressed opposition to his wife's wearing a chaddari. At age five, while watching a military parade with her father, General Nazari decided on her course in life.

General Nazari was serving as a police officer at the beginning of the Soviet invasion. She sent her husband abroad to protect him while she remained in Afghanistan with their three small children. He returned many years later, but she had decided that she did not want a husband. She continued to invest in her career and served as a role model for women. She expressed concern with the current direction of her country, and asked why organizations

General Aziza Nazari, Afghan police officer (supplied by Lina Abirafeh, October 12, 2002; used with permission).

were not working with men. She explained: "It is not only women who need help. In Afghanistan you may think that women don't know anything and men do. But this is not the case. Both need help."

When asked about women's security issues and the prevalence of violence against women, she strongly stated that violence against women has increased recently because men are having difficulties dealing with changes in women's rights and status. She elaborated: "In all the world, violence against women is increasing, not just in Afghanistan. But we are Muslim people and we need to study gender issues and women's rights in the context of Islam and society in Afghanistan."

General Nazari explained that the large international presence has prevented women in Afghanistan from defining their rights for themselves. Furthermore, it has created resentment with men who feel that their own issues are not addressed. Even in the context of violence, she explained, violence against men and violence against women by other women are unacknowledged problems and are never discussed. She elaborated that the international community only talks about women's rights in relationship to men. General Nazari put it this way: "Women and women! That's what the men say. This makes difficulties and problems in families because all men hear from the outside is 'women and women.' They no longer know where they fit."

On the concept of gender, General Nazari explained: "'Gender' has not had a chance to define itself in Afghanistan. It is unknown here and does not translate. People think gender is brought from other countries and doesn't belong to Afghanistan. But when we say equality of men and women, then the people say 'Yes. This is in Islam. Yes. This is in the Constitution.' But 'gender,' this is foreign to us still. In this society, it is difficult for people to accept changes so quickly."

Part II: Voices of Afghan Women Political Leaders

Except when the Taliban ruled, women in Afghanistan have been involved in public life.[16] After the Taliban were overthrown in 2001, women increased their participation in government in numbers and importance. These profiles provide images of but a few of the women in government.

Dr. Habiba Sarabi, Governor of Bamiyan

Governor Habiba Sarabi holds the distinction of being the first woman to ever be the governor of a province in Afghanistan. President Karzai appointed Sarabi governor of Bamiyan on March 2, 2005. Before she was appointed governor, she served as vice president of Humanitarian Assistance for Women and Children of Afghanistan and served as minister of women's affairs in the transitional government from June 2002 to October 2004.[17]

Habiba Sarabi, Afghan minister of Women's Affairs in her Kabul office. She later became governor of Bamiyan Province (AFP Photo).

In a 2008 interview, Governor Sarabi was asked: "How does being the first female governor in the history of Afghanistan make you feel, especially since Bamiyan is extremely impoverished and one of the least developed provinces in the country? What are some of the challenges you face as a female governor of Bamiyan?"[18] Sarabi replied, "There are a lot of challenges, yet I feel that in such a society women can do something. The first step is for women to be active. I am happy that there is no one saying that women cannot be.... No one can stop women from going ahead in Afghan society. Of course, there are many challenges in front of us. Like you said, Bamiyan is very poor and the fact that society is male-dominated makes my job even more difficult."[19]

When asked, "What are the biggest challenges for a female statesman in a patriarchal society?" She replied, "It is very difficult. We have to be patient with the people so that they may eventually accept our policies, otherwise we will face even more difficulties. Our ideas also have to be complete, taking into account the past and the future. In addition, when we talk we need to be strong, or the people will not listen.[20]

Sarabi's background is impressive. She studied in India with a World Health Organization fellowship and is a graduate of the Pharmacology Department of Kabul University. She was a teacher for girls in underground schools during the Taliban control. In 1998, she became a member and later general manager of the Afghanistan Institute of Learning, an organization that works to provide women with basic education. Habiba Sarabi was born in Mazar-e-Sharif, Afghanistan, in 1956.[21]

In a 2002 interview, when Sarabi was the minister of culture and education, she said that the situation of women had changed. Many Afghan women believed that they could play an active role in the future of the country. Women were going to schools and universities, and had begun to work. She recognized that addressing women's concerns would take time:

> The transition government is trying to create democratic rules to be able to guarantee rights and liberties to women, but this cannot happen in a short time — especially while there continue to be people who are opposed to these changes for all women. And these differences arise more forcefully in connection with women who live outside the principal cities, where opportunities for employment and education diminish.[22]

Sarabi also recognized challenges, one being that there are not enough schools for girls. Another is the problem of early marriages. She advocated meeting these challenges by raising compulsory schooling to sixteen years of age in all provinces.

Bamiyan is a peaceful province. It is not threatened by lack of security, but it is hampered by harsh winter conditions, irregular electricity and unpaved roads. Bamiyan's accomplishments have been advanced by Sarabi's leadership. In 2008, approximately 45 percent of the girls attend school, up from almost none in 2001.

In 2001, according to the Bamiyan education department, there were 115 schools which educated about 20,000 mostly male students. Most of these schools lacked dedicated buildings. In 2008, about 58,000 boys and 38,000 girls are students at 301 schools, 157 of which have dedicated buildings.[23]

Sarabi acknowledged that Bamiyan is underdeveloped and that its people are very poor. So she has developed a ten-year strategy plan from

2005 to 2015 to reconstruct the province. The plan focuses on infrastructure, security, tourism, agriculture, education and health.[24]

Sarabi faces challenges to develop Bamiyan's historical sites which would encourage tourism. Some citizens are uneducated or illiterate and do not see the value in doing so, and in many cases, people are so poor that their first concern is food.[25] Bamiyan, the site of an early Buddhist monastery, has many statues of Buddha carved into the sides of cliffs facing Bamiyan city. The two most prominent were standing Buddhas, known as the Buddhas of Bamiyan. They were cultural landmarks for many years and are listed among UNESCO's World Heritage Sites. In March 2001, the Taliban decreed the statues as idolatrous, ordered them to be demolished, and they were destroyed.[26]

In a 2005 interview with BBC, Sarabi was asked whether she felt the weight of responsibility as Afghanistan's first female governor. She responded, "Yeah, if someone in my position would be a man it would be more easy for them to be accepted as a governor." But BBC believes that Habiba Sarabi is climbing the mountains that are higher than they would be for men, and that she is one of the "gifted women in Afghanistan emerging from the destruction and intolerance that is all around."[27]

Husn Banu Ghazanfar:
Minister of Women's Affairs

Husn Banu Ghazanfar brings an accomplished background to her position as minister for the Ministry of Women's Affairs. She was sworn in by President Karzai on May 2, 2006. In 2003, she was appointed as the head of the literature faculty at Kabul University and held this post until she was appointed minister. In addition, she has been a member of the following organizations: High Council of the Ministry of Higher Education, Speranto International Association of Women, International Association of Turk Zabanan and Board of Directors of Hakim Naser Khesro Balkhi Association.[28]

In 2006, Ghazanfar said in an interview, "We've had three decades of war in Afghanistan, which have had very bad consequences for women.... It takes time to solve these problems." She explained that the most pressing issues facing women were violence and their low education levels, particularly in the rural areas. Ghazanfar said that she hoped that all Afghan women one day would have access to education. As to her own position, she said, "It's not important which position I have, but it's more important that I'm working for women — the most needy women of the world.... I'm really happy here, working for the women of Afghanistan."[29]

In her policy against violence, Ghazanfar states,

> It is our responsibility to inform communities about the unpleasant outcomes of the incidents of violence against women which end in tragedies, suicides and cases of putting oneself on fire so that the storm of anger and violence will not destroy the pleasant family environment. Try to prevent forced and early marriages. Try to tell each and every one out in the society to be kind with their daughters and females, family and society members and do not quarrel with them so that they are not condemned in the history.[30]

Basing her philosophy in the teachings of Islam, she also speaks out against all types of inhumanity. But she stresses, "Afghan women are that fraction of the society that has suffered the most."[31]

At the same time, she believes there is a necessity to keep in mind gender roles and family integrity: "Gender roles are based on division of working place and authority among men and women [and] family integrity should be kept in mind. The culture of Afghans is based on honor and dignity, which is reflected through women's deeds."[32]

The list of accomplishments of the Ministry of Women's Affairs is lengthy,[33] but in 2008, Afghanistan launched two new women's rights programs: "Healthy Family, Happy Society" and "Law and Women." The purpose of these campaigns is to eliminate violence against women and promote women's rights. Ghazanfar, said the Healthy Family, Happy Society campaign will be carried out by religious leaders in several provinces to promote awareness of women's rights. The second program, Law and Women, will be run by lawyers and prosecutors. "Lawyers and prosecutors will, by publishing posters and launching informative campaigns, highlight the right of women envisaged in the country's constitution and guaranteed by Islam,"[34] she said.

Ghazanfar speaks fluently in Dari, Pashto, Uzbek and Russian, and has some knowledge of the Turkish and English languages. She has published scientific articles and essays in national and international newspa-

Husn Banu Ghazanfar (second from left), Afghan Women's Affairs minister, and Dr. Gisela Hayfa (fourth from left), director general of GTZ, signing a memorandum at the Women's Affairs Ministry, Kabul (Zuhra Najwa/Pajhwok/MAXPPP — Kabul 2007/01/25).

pers. She also writes poetry and literary works. She has written *The Human Fate: Predations in the 21st Century* and *The Secrets of Beauty and Attraction*, and has translated the book *Self Realization*.[35]

Ghazanfar was born in Balkh on February 1, 1957. She graduated from Sultan Razia High School in Mazar-e-sharif and received her B.A. and master's degrees in literature and sociology from Stawarpool Qafqaaz in 1983. She then worked as part of the literature faculty at Kabul University. After two years of service as a lecturer there, she went to Petersburg where she earned a doctorate in philology.[36]

Ghazanfar is not married and has no children. But she was sequestered in her home during the reign of the Taliban (late 1990s to 2001).[37]

Zahida Ansary: Afghan Ambassador to the Republic of Bulgaria and Non-resident Ambassador to the Republic of Macedonia

On September 8, 2005, President Karzai appointed Zahida Ansary as Afghan ambassador to the Republic of Bulgaria and non-resident ambas-. sador to the Republic of Macedonia. Ansary is one of two female ambassadors. The other is Maliha Zulfacar, Afghan ambassador to Germany.[38] Shortly after her appointment Ansary said,

> Afghan women proved in a short time ... not only on a national level but internationally, too, that they can take part in political activities.... In diplomacy, too, there is no problem [for women to handle the jobs]. You know that an ambassador's job, as the representative of the president, is to defend government policy and the rights of citizens in a foreign country within international law. It is a very important job and a big responsibility.[39]

Five months after 9/11, Ansary returned to the Ministry of Foreign Affairs and was appointed as the director of the Fifth Political Department where she conducted the affairs related to diplomatic representatives of Afghanistan to the United States, Canada and other American countries. In addition, she was a member of the Presidential Electoral Commission, a member of the Joint Electoral Management Body and a member of the Electoral Law Subcommittee.[40]

On February 27, 2008, Ansary was awarded with the honorary decoration of the Ministry of Foreign Affairs of Bulgaria, the "Golden Laurel Branch." H. E. Feim Chaushev, deputy minister of foreign affairs of the Republic of Bulgaria, on behalf of H. E. Ivaylo Kalfin, deputy prime minister and minister of foreign affairs, presented the honor "for her contribution to the development of bilateral relations between Afghanistan and Bulgaria."[41] The award was presented at the occasion of the end of Ansary's mandate as ambassador of Afghanistan to Bulgaria.[42]

Prior to her appointment, Ansary had worked with the Ministry of Foreign Affairs since 1992 and with the Ministry of Finance since 1977. She also worked in the presidency of Government Control and Inspections for a two-year period.[43]

Ansary was educated at Rabia Balkhi High School in Kabul and "Faculty of Law and Political Sciences at Kabul University." She and her husband, Dr. Azam Ansary, have two young adult children, a son, Riaz Ansary, and a daughter, Hawa Ansary.[44]

On September 6, 2007, Ansary spoke at a celebration of the 800th anniversary of the birth of thirteenth-century Maulana Jallaludin Balkhi Rumi. She reflected his message to the humanity of all times: "You are what you are thinking. The remaining is your body, consisting of bones, muscles and the like."[45] This message, she said,

> is saying that the essence of human being has a limitless greatness. If the human thoughts are of an infinite world of varieties and diversities, unified by the general unity of love, knowledge and all beauties of life, the life [on] earth becomes heavenly, full of freedom, full of joy and happiness.[46]

She outlines the progress Afghanistan has made: "The legitimacy of our newly founded institutions is gradually taking roots; our society is brimming with freedom and activity. Thousands of kilometers of highways, thousands of schools, clinics, hospitals, communication systems, water and energy networks, and many other projects have been completed and they are all common achievements [that we] deserve to care about."[47]

But the progress must be made secure against the threat of terrorism, Ansary says. She persuasively calls upon the famous philosopher poet of the late nineteenth and early twentieth centuries, Alama Iqbal, who once beautifully portrayed Afghanistan, writing:

> Asia is of earth and
> Of waters a body
> But the country of Afghans
> Has the position of the heart
> In this body
> Its depravity is
> The depravity of the Asia
> Its prosperity is
> The prosperity of the Asia.[48]

The great Iqbal gave an accurate perception of Afghanistan for that time, said Ansary, adding, "But now ... all can see that Afghanistan is the heart of the entire globe, particularly in terms of security. If Afghanistan is secure, the entire globe is secure. If Afghanistan is insecure, the whole world is insecure because the fate of our security is intertwined."[49]

John Beyrle, U.S. ambassador to Bulgaria (second from left), at a round-
table discussion organized by the Atlantic Club in Sofia on July 19, 2007,
with Zahida Ansary, Afghanistan ambassador to Bulgaria (far right), and
Russian embassy representatives, Bulgarian politicians, officers and jour-
nalists who also took part in the discussion (U.S. Embassy in Bulgaria).

Maliha Zulfacar:
Afghan Ambassador to Germany

Her Excellency Maliha Zulfacar is the Afghan ambassador to Germany. Of her appointment Zulfacar said, "It is a great honor for me. With
that honor comes much responsibility. Having been the first woman
appointed as an ambassador from Afghanistan gives me the opportunity
to serve my country of birth and also to demonstrate that when Afghan
women are given the chance for education, they too will be able to par-
ticipate effectively in the reconstruction of the country."[50] At the time of
her appointment, Zulfacar was a professor of sociology at California Poly-
technic State University, San Luis Obispo. From 2001 to 2006 Zulfacar
spent the academic year teaching at the university and organizing activities and fund-raisers for Afghanistan. She spent her summers teaching
social science and establishing programs at Kabul University.[51] After the

fall of the Taliban, she was the substitutional minister for higher education in the Afghan Transitional Government.[52]

One of her accomplishments was the production of the film *Kabul Transit*, which was shown in Amsterdam at a major international film festival. Zulfacar says, "It is about daily life in Kabul, about all the changes that have taken place since 2001, about people's perspectives."[53] Zulfacar has also collected interviews for publication, to produce what she says is all too rare: a history of Afghanistan as told by Afghans.[54] In 2001, her first film, *Guftago: Dialog with an Afghan Village*, documented her trip with an international delegation of women who toured mountain villages in 2000.[55]

The position of ambassador is challenging in that 100,000 Afghan refugees live in Germany, the highest number of Afghan refugees in all of Europe, says Zulfacar. A second challenge is how to utilize Germany, a key country in the reconstruction of Afghanistan, to expand and reactivate some of the historical cooperation that exists with Germany.[56]

In Afghanistan, the people would like to see more tangible results from large sums of money that have been designated for the reconstruction. Zulfacar says, "Many changes have taken place, however they are changes that do not reach the livelihood of ordinary Afghans."[57] These desired tangible changes include electricity and running water.

Maliha Zulfacar was born in Kabul. After her graduation from Rabia Balkhi High School in Kabul, she left Afghanistan to study in the United States. Upon her return to Afghanistan, she taught sociology at Kabul University. As a young mother she left Afghanistan in 1979, the year the Soviets invaded. She escaped through Germany and in 1985 settled in California. She has two children. In 1988, she joined the Cal Poly Social Sciences Department, teaching ethnic studies. She earned her doctorate in sociology from Paderborn University in Germany in 1997. Zulfacar is fluent in Dari, Pashtu, German, English and Arabic.[58]

Fatima Gailani: Head of the Afghan Red Crescent Society (Red Cross)

In January 2005, President Karzai appointed Fatima Gailani as president and general secretary of the Afghan Red Crescent Society (ARCS). The ARCS is a member of the International Federation of the Red Cross/Red Crescent Societies and works in thirty-one out of thirty-two provinces. Gailani's first priority is to reestablish frameworks for reconstruction that have been fractured by the long war. The overall objective is to provide disaster relief, basic health care and resource development to all citizens, including millions of refugees.[59]

According to Fatima Gailani, women and children are often the first victims of war. Among the most vulnerable, she says, are disabled parents, people who are mentally challenged because of the war, and young widows. She believes that there are too many vulnerable people and estimates their number at about 60 percent of the Afghan population. While she believes that it is not possible to provide help to more than half a country, she says,

> My hope is that one day, we will be able to say that we managed to help some of the most vulnerable people by bringing them into Red Crescent homes for the destitute, known as Marastoon. I want to give them some hope, not only in their hearts but their minds as well. Children living in Marastoon are given free education and they can learn a [vocation], like tailoring or carpet weaving.[60]

As a teenager, Gailani volunteered in the Red Crescent following the example of her mother and grandmother. She assisted the organization in fund-raising before the war. She is the daughter of Pir Sayed Ahmed Gailani, the leader of the National Islamic Front of Afghanistan, who fought against the Soviet occupation in the 1980s. She speaks of her childhood as one of privilege and equality between men and women. Her mother, the wife of a religious leader, taught that there is responsibility in privilege. Gailani graduated from Malalai High School in Kabul and earned a B.A. and an M.A. in Persian literature and Sufism in 1978 from the National University of Iran. She also earned an MA in Islamic studies from the Muslim College in London in 1994. In 1979 her family began living in exile in England. Life as a refugee was life without privilege. During this time, she was spokesperson in London for the Afghan mujahedeen. She attended the Bonn Conference on Afghanistan in 2001. After her return to Afghanistan in 2002, she was chosen as a delegate to the Emergency Loya Jirga — Grand Council — of June 2002. She was appointed as a constitution-drafting and -ratifying commissioner. Gailani is the author of two books, *Mosques of London* and a biography of Mohammed Mosa Shafi.[61]

Gailani's goal is to bring more women into the Red Crescent. She believes that the greatest challenge to women is familial, saying, "In most parts of this country women face the exact same discrimination they faced five years ago. This discrimination does not come from the government ... it comes from their own families."[62] Although Gailani doesn't think about her gender, she works to sensitize families. She says, "I think when you reach a certain level of education, people will respect you. But the dilemma is how to encourage fathers, brothers and families to give this chance to their daughters. Whenever I get compliments from men from various tribes, I reply to them by saying, 'If you want your daughter to be like me, then you have to give her the same opportunities that my father gave me.'"[63]

When asked by the *International Review of the Red Cross* whether the role of the Afghan women is evolving, she replied,

> We cannot achieve peace, human rights, women's rights or democracy with imported rules and regulations. It wouldn't be sensible. The presence of foreigners, of foreign troops, the influence of the UN, can temporarily bring changes for women. But are these changes really fundamental? Do they have roots in our society and our culture? I do not think so. That's why I insist upon an Afghan solution, which means involving religious and tribal leaders and ordinary village people. In order to establish an Afghan feminism, we have to involve our own religion and culture.[64]

Nasrine Abou-Bakre Gross: Founder, Roqia Center for Women's Rights, Studies and Education in Afghanistan

Nasrine Abou-Bakre Gross had finished her first year of law and political science at Kabul University when she was awarded a U.S. Agency for International Development scholarship to study at American University of Beirut. She left her native Afghanistan for Lebanon to attend the university in 1965 as one of the second generation of educated women in Afghanistan. She received her B.A. in education in 1970. She left Lebanon for the United States in 1971 and returned to Afghanistan in 2001.[65]

In 1992, Gross began research that culminated in 1998 when she published her first book, *Memories of the First Girls' High School*. She says, "I thought that would be a good way to get back to Afghanistan mentally

143

and revisit the time I was growing up in Afghanistan in my high school."[66] Her second book, *Steps of Peace and Our Responsibility*, brought her contacts with different ethnic groups through experts on their cultures.

Gross says that when the Taliban came in 1996, she had an introduction or reentry to Afghan society. The coming of the Taliban motivated her to activism. "Within two weeks of the Taliban coming to Afghanistan, they had created a fire in the state, [and] with that kind of fire, I couldn't sit still. My mind couldn't be still."[67]

In 2001, she was part of the group that wrote "The Declaration of the Essential Rights of Afghan Women" in Dushambe, Tajikistan. Also in that year she took a group of American women to the free part of Afghanistan where, unknowingly, they went sightseeing with and stayed in the same guest house as the two terrorists who, while they were there, killed Ahmad Shah Massoud on the ninth of September. Two days later, 9/11 happened, which was a major turning point for Gross. She says, "I realized how abandoned, how forgotten, and how terribly deprived my people were and had been for years. I wanted to dedicate my life to Afghanistan from then on for the well-being of Afghanistan."[68]

Nasrine Abou-Bakre Gross (2008), founder, the Roqia Center for Women's Rights, Studies and Education in Afghanistan, an officially registered Afghan civil society organization that aims to assist the cause of women as an integral part of the country's democratization and reconstruction (photograph courtesy Nasrine Abou-Bakre Gross, 2008).

Fortunately, says Gross, America got involved, and she was invited to attend the transfer of power in December 2001. Since that day, she has lived in Afghanistan. She participated in the Loya Jirga of Afghan Women in Brussels in November 2001. In 2002, she worked for the representation of women on the Emergency Loya Jirga.[69]

In 2003, Gross worked vigorously for the constitutional Loya Jirga by helping organize 130 conferences for women inside of Afghanistan. She helped collect 300,000 signatures worldwide for the revision of the constitution. She jokes that this is comparable to about eighty pounds of paper. Since they didn't have enough money to bring all the signatures from the United States and Europe, they gave the Revision Commission 100,000 signatures. Gross and other women worked to have the equal rights clause included. Her goal was to "reinstitute a constitution that is totally democratic and recognizes all the inalienable rights of its citizens regardless of gender, for both men and women."[70] She says,

> With ratification of the constitution, I thought my part of my mission had been accomplished. And by no means, was I the only woman that worked on this. I am very glad to be a member of that large group of Afghan women.
> Politically speaking, that deals a blow at the heart of the Taliban philosophy and tells the world that Afghanistan is not afraid of the terrorism of the Taliban. That is one of their missions: create terror and fear.[71]
> Even though six and a half years have passed since the liberation of Afghanistan, I still think the cause of Afghan women today is as relevant. It doesn't have to seem an immediately tragic face, but nonetheless the women of Afghanistan are the defining success against terrorism and extremism and philosophies like the Taliban.[72]

In 2004 Gross wrote a book about the parliamentary elections in Afghanistan, *Women's Guide to Winning in 2005*, that she used as a basis for a seminar which yielded some funds.[73] The funding enabled her to go to six cities to gather all of the female candidates for parliament, regardless of their political affiliation, from about fourteen provinces for training.[74] Gross's initial work before 2003 with women involved conferences to get signatures, and explanations of what constituted women's rights. When the first Afghan presidential election was being planned, Gross helped educate women on what makes a democracy.

After women got elected to the parliament, Gross joined an organization with non–Afghan women whose purpose was to take each of the ninety-one female members of Parliament at least once to a successful parliament in a city elsewhere in the world. This program began by taking thirty women to Paris in 2006. In 2007, the organization took twenty women to the Islamic parliament in Turkey. In 2008, provided funds are available, the group hopes to bring another twenty women to the U.S. Congress.[75]

One of Gross's many accomplishments is the founding of the Roqia Center for Women's Rights, Studies and Education in Afghanistan, an officially registered Afghan civil society organization. The center's purpose is "to assist the cause of women as an integral part of the country's democratization and reconstruction."[76] The activities of the center focus on rights, studies and education. As a partner to the center, Gross created a U.S.–based nonprofit organization, Kabultec, to maximize the center's effectiveness in other areas, such as fund-raising.

Since 2001, Nasrine Abou-Bakre Gross has lived in Afghanistan, but visits her family in the United States part of each year. She is a member of the Kabul University faculty and has taught courses there for five years. She is also involved in nine research projects whose results are published in the Dari language. During the time she visits in the United States, her schedule is demanding. She gives speeches, writes grant proposals, seeks new donors, searches for volunteers to go to Afghanistan, and raises funds to help the country.[77] Of her multi-dimensional work, Gross says, "My most meaningful activity is working with and for the women of Afghanistan. I want to make sure that we have ... [a] new generation of Afghan women who can be good leaders, who can be good advocates, who can be good decision makers.... To me, success in Afghanistan, however we define it, can no longer be excluding women.[78]

Sima Samar, Chairperson of the Afghanistan Independent Human Rights Commission (AIHRC) and United Nations Special Rapporteur on the Situation of Human Rights in Sudan

The Global Health Council awarded Dr. Sima Samar the 2004 Jonathan Mann Award for Health and Human Rights for her work in human rights for girls and women in Afghanistan. Samar was also awarded the John F. Kennedy Profile in Courage Award. In 2002, Samar became the first women's affairs minister in the interim government. Male colleagues taunted her, and she began to receive death threats from Islamic conservatives. Ultimately, she was forced to step down from her cabinet post. Samar was appointed to the noncabinet position of chair of the Afghanistan Independent Human Rights Commission. Since 2005, she has been the United Nations Special Rapporteur on the Situation of Human Rights in Sudan. Samar's accomplishments are numerous and outstanding. She founded and directs the Shuhada Organization, the oldest Afghan and the largest nongovernmental organization led by women that operates in the region. She is also Afghanistan's first minister of women's affairs.[79]

Previous to her position as chair of the Commission, she was elected as the vice chair of the emergency *loya jirga* in 2002, chosen as the first deputy chair and minister of women's affairs in the interim administration of Afghanistan at the Bonn meeting in 2001 and received the John Humphrey Freedom Award in 2001.[80]

Sima Samar was born February 4, 1957, in Jaghoori, Ghazni province. She obtained her degree in medicine in February 1982 from Kabul University. Dr. Samar's husband was arrested during the Soviet occupation, forcing her to flee to Pakistan with her young son. Her husband was never heard

Sima Samar, UN Human Rights Council Special Rapporteur in Sudan, speaks to reporters regarding the human rights situation in Darfur during a press conference in Khartoum, August 2, 2007 (Isam Al-Haj/AFP/Getty Images).

from again.[81] Dr. Samar is known for dangerous pursuits under the Taliban regime. Unwilling to be deterred, she opened ten Afghan clinics and four hospitals for women and children, set up schools in rural Afghanistan for more than 17,000 students, founded a hospital and school for refugee girls in Pakistan, established literacy programs and distributed food aid and information on hygiene and family planning. Her philosophy, "I've always been in danger, but I don't mind.... I believe we will die one day so I said let's take the risk and help somebody else."[82]

In 2004, estimates were that over 36,700 girls and boys studied in the Shuhada schools that she founded. The clinics and hospitals she opened provide services to some 750 patients per day.[83] In 2007, Samar ranked #92 on *Forbes'* list of the 100 most powerful women in the world. At a regional conference, Samar discussed the increasing number of cases of self-immolation of women or suicide by fire who are forced into marriage and suffer chronic abuse. Samar said, "It is the final decision for women who don't have any other way to solve their problems."[84] In 2006, she ranked #28 out of the 100 most powerful women in the world. At a speech at Brown University that year, Samar cautioned: "Women's rights and human rights will not be real unless there is enough security and law enforcement in the country."[85]

Samar stated three reasons for the violence: failure to fulfill promises to improve security; impunity enjoyed by human rights violators; and lack of law enforcement and the war economy. She explains that none of the warring sides have respected the human rights of women. The world condemns the extreme violators, the Taliban, but she says, "we cannot forget that the Taliban were removed from power in retaliation for the 9/11 terrorist attack on the United States and not to restore women's rights and human rights."[86] She believes that although the women's rights situation now is somewhat better than it has been in the last two decades and that progress for women was made in the new constitution, women's lives have improved little, particularly in conservative areas.

Yet Samar perseveres in her philosophy that there is hope in the work to be done and left her audience at Brown University with this thought: "Sometimes I think of the world as a bird. If a wing or a country is broken, the bird cannot fly. As a global community, we are all responsible for treating the bird so that it will fly."[87]

Samar continues to add to her numerous awards. In January 2008, she was given the accolade as One of a Different View's 15 Champions of World Democracy.[88]

Massouda Jalal, Minister of Women's Affairs, First Female Candidate for President of Afghanistan

Massouda Jalal was one of three women ministers out of the twenty-seven appointed to the cabinet in December 2004 and will serve until 2009. The other two women were Sediqa Balkhi, minister of Martyrs and Disabled, and Amina Afzali, minister of Youth Affairs. Jalal was appointed minister of Women's Affairs. Jalal, a medical doctor, was also President Karzai's only female opponent in the October 9, 2004, presidential election.[89] As a 41-year-old mother of three, Jalal made history as the first ever Afghan woman to run for president.[90] Jalal's presidential campaign lacked funds and was supported largely by students. She had no bodyguard and ran on a platform that was pro-democracy and anti-warlord. Her campaign was headquartered in a borrowed flat marked with bullet holes

in a run-down suburb of Kabul.[91] Jalal received 1.1 percent of the vote in the election. She placed sixth out of seventeen male candidates. An exit poll showed Jalal received about seven percent of the vote among Afghan women.[92]

Afghan Minister of Women's Affairs Massouda Jalal attends a March 11, 2005, discussion to talk about the future of Afghanistan and give her assessment on the recent and upcoming elections in Afghanistan, at the Middle East Institute in Washington, D.C. Jalal is best known for being the only female candidate who ran against Afghan President Hamid Karzai in the October 2004 presidential elections (TIM SLOAN/AFP/Getty Images).

Bravery has always been an attribute of Jalal. She showed her courage as a pediatrician in Kabul during the civil war in the 1990s and when she ran the United Nations High Commissioner for Refugees' office under the Taliban. The Taliban forced her to wear a burqa and jailed her at one time for a few days. She also worked for the World Food Program, responsible for gender issues and health.[93]

Jalal's candidacy for president angered fundamentalists, but she was not intimidated. "If I show weakness some men will say, 'look she is not brave.' They will say, 'there is another woman who gave up.'"[94] She believed Afghanistan was ready for a female president. To the question of when the country will have gender equality, she answered, "If I am elected.... If not, perhaps in another century."[95]

As minister of Women's Affairs, Jalal shares her vision of leadership:

> Leadership of women is not just a matter of mandate. Women's leadership has to be bought with a clear vision, fired by commitment, nourished by credibility, galvanized by performance, and cradled incessantly in the bosom of power. It should stand in the bedrock of a politicized constituency, and a platform of results that would benefit not only women, but everyone in society.[96]

However, Jalal describes the leadership of women in the reconstruction process "a distant reality and the road is paved with daunting obstacles."[97] The challenge is complex, but she gives five ways to begin:

- Invest in rebuilding of women's human resource [health];

- Get the support of men;

- Develop a new concept of power and train women for leadership;

- Transform culture and make institutions women-friendly; and

- Fight poverty and violence.[98]

Jalal was born January 5, 1962, in Gul Bahar in Kapisa Province. She is one of seven children. After attending high school in Kabul, she attended Kabul University, where she was a member of the faculty until 1996 when the Taliban removed her. Her husband is a law instructor at Kabul University; they have three children.[99]

7

The Future

There is a window of opportunity for all Afghans to go in the right direction ... as soon as we are able to establish institutions that are needed for the country, that will help.
— Dr. Zahir Tanin, ambassador and permanent representative
of Afghanistan to the United Nations.[1]

President Hamid Karzai credits the resilience and unfailing people of Afghanistan and the generous support of the international community for the great strides the country has made toward peace, stability and democracy. In spite of the achievements, Karzai realizes the journey will be long and challenges remain.[2] The Friedrich-Ebert-Stiftung (FES) political foundation's 2005 *Gender Report* reflects Karzai's sentiments, stating, "There are no quick fixes to development concerns, gender issues, and over twenty years of conflict in Afghanistan."[3]

Ultimately, lasting peace and security will depend on "building effective and capable institutions of governance," Karzai says.[4] The president has expressed gratitude for what the international community has done for Afghanistan and to the soldiers and workers who gave their precious lives, alongside the Afghans, in service to the country. He reminds us that global security is a benefit to all community members.

Ambassador Zahir Tanin, permanent representative of Afghanistan to the United Nations, believes that security is critical, saying, "As long as we are able to strengthen the institutions, Afghanistan will emerge as a very different country."[5]

The FES *Gender Report*, authored by Dr. Lina Abirafeh, says that post-conflict circumstances bring opportunities for new roles for women and men. The report insightfully states, "Gender roles could change while gender relations might remain the same."[6] The report explains that undertakings to promote strategic interests may contribute to changes, while projects meeting practical needs may not necessarily affect the status quo. In addition, it recommends that the focus of gender include men as well as women so that neither group feels marginalized, but that gender mainstreaming should be combined with a focus on women. This way mainstreaming keeps a gender perspective and women may still benefit from increased opportunities toward equity. Perhaps some advantages can result because in conflict and post-conflict states gender roles are changing and may be renegotiated.[7] In a journal article written in 2007, Abirafeh again expresses a negative result of female-focused interventions, saying that "the particular focus on women in Afghanistan ... has actually been detrimental from the perspective of Afghan men and women."[8]

The Ministry of Women's Affairs in Afghanistan holds a similar position, saying that

> the issue of gender relations should be studied from the traditional and cultural dimension of the people of Afghanistan, which is a patriarchy (men predominant) culture. It should be understood that family is the structural unit of the society, from which relatives and tribe are developed. Most of the women of Afghanistan don't want to be isolated from their families and lose their family integrity.... Most men, especially in rural areas, are satisfied with these roles and responsibilities and relations.[9]

Fatima Gailani, head of the Afghan Red Crescent, agrees with this concept, saying that imported rules and explanations will only temporarily achieve peace or women's rights. Permanent solutions must be rooted in Afghan culture. "I insist upon an Afghan solution," she says, "which means involving religious and tribal leaders and ordinary village people. In order to establish an Afghan feminism, we have to involve our own religion and culture."[10]

The voices and images of Afghan women and men in chapter 6 echo the position of these leaders, with such phrases as "This is Afghanistan, those things just don't work here." General Aziza Nazari's voice also reflects the same idea when she says "we need to study gender issues and women's rights in the context of Islam and society in Afghanistan."[11]

Ambassador Haron Amin adds that Afghanistan needs to include all members of the Afghan society in the development in the country:

> Any country that wants to have a chance at the future, any country that wants to have an opportunity at economic equity, any country that wants to have all segments of society to be constructive elements within that country: these countries are states where they recognize the rights of every individual. In Afghanistan, President Hamid Karzai and those, especially the younger generation of people like myself, that are working with President Karzai, are of the firm conviction that without enabling every segment of society, but particularly ... the women of Afghanistan who comprise more than 50 percent of the population ... Afghanistan will not attain development. We will be subject to economic deprivation, we will be subject to lack of development, we will be subject to violence and other acts that will, in the ultimate consequence, put us back to being victimized by the Taliban or like-minded agenda.[12]

Amin believes, against the ominous era of terror of the Taliban, against the draconian models of the Taliban, that Afghanistan is gradually achieving fundamental rights, for example, of education, of life with liberty and freedom of expression, of life not only for men but also for women. He adds, "It is a struggle. It will take time. But the longer we have people with us, the sooner we can achieve those objectives."[13]

Amin concludes that as long as Afghanistan has segments of society deprived of their fundamental rights, the country will not attain development in the true sense. But, says,

> "I hope that the international community recognizes that sometimes granting rights is easier, but fulfilling those rights, ensuring those rights is more difficult. [I hope for] them to bear this juncture, for them to be with us in the transition, and for us ultimately to be the basic victors ... against infringement of all fundamental human rights."[14]

Tanin reminds us that inequalities and things such as violence against women are caused by different forces. Tradition sometimes is the main reason for the unequal treatment of women, rather than the Taliban or other like forces. He says, "Sometimes it is a source of income for them to marry their daughters to a wealthy man.... I'm certain that we can change the situation, but I am not sure how long it will take. It may take five years or ten years to achieve something, but when we achieve something, there are a lot others to be achieved."[15]

Amin believes that achievement in and of itself is remarkable. "The significant thing is that the level of achievements in Afghanistan is breathtaking, they're very promising. [We have] the history of human suffering and then the recovery from those sufferings. I think this is a very promising story. We are only five years into it. I think in ten years time Afghanistan will be a driving force, not only in Afghanistan ... but [regionally].[16]

We must listen to the voices and see the images of Afghan men and women, leaders and citizens, and proceed to help Afghanistan based on their ideas and their culture. We should keep foremost in mind that the country has endured nearly twenty-five years of conflict, and that it can advance more should security be in place. Within a safe country, its government and other institutions can flourish. With improvements in this context, Afghan woman and men will experience better lives.

Acronyms and Glossary

AIHRC — Afghanistan Independent Human Rights Commission

ANSO — Afghanistan NGO Safety Office

BPHS — Basic Package of Health Services

CEDAW — International Convention on the Elimination of All Forms of Discrimination Against Women

CPI — Corruption Perceptions Index

CRC — United Nations Convention on the Rights of the Child

EFA — Education for All. As the lead agency, UNESCO has been mandated to coordinate the international efforts to reach Education for All.

EPHS — Essential Package of Hospital Services

GDI — Gender Development Index (adjusts the HDI average to reflect the inequalities between men and women in the same three dimensions: a long and healthy life, knowledge, and a decent standard of living)

GDP — Gross Domestic Product (a way of measuring the health of the economy, it represents the total dollar value of all goods and services produced over a specific time period)

GER — Gross Enrollment Ratio

GPI — gender parity index

HDI — Human Development Index (a composite indicator that measures education, longevity, and economic performance)

HPI — Human Poverty Index (focuses on deprivations, specifically those that limit a long and healthy life, a decent standard of living, and lack of knowledge or exclusion from the world of reading and communication)

ICCPR — International Covenant on Civil and Political Rights

IDA — International Development Association

IDPs — internally displaced persons

ISAF — International Security Assistance Force of NATO

Jamaat Ulama-e Islam— pro–Taliban party and Pakistan's largest Islamist movement

jihadi— participants in Islamic holy war

Loya Jirga— the Grand Assembly (the traditional method Afghans have used throughout history to solve their political issues)

madrasas— Islamic schools

MDGs— Millennium Development Goals

Meshrano Jirga— upper house of Loya Jirga

MoE— Ministry of Education

MoWA— Ministry of Women's Affairs

mujahedeen— freedom fighters (Pakistan-based Islamic party); any Muslim who fights a jihad

NATO— North Atlantic Treaty Organization

NGOs— Non-governmental Organizations

NSP— National Solidary Program

RAWA— Revolutionary Association of the Women of Afghanistan

Ring Road network— a highway under construction that loops the rugged mountain terrain and sparsely populated countryside to connect to the major cities

SGBV— sexual and gender-based violence

Shari'a— body of Islamic religious law based in part on the Koran (the religious text of Islam), hadith (sayings of Muhammad), and on precedent.

TBA— Traditional Birth Attendant

UNESCO— United Nations Educational, Scientific and Cultural Organization

UNFPA— United Nations Population Fund

UNHCHR— United Nations High Commissioner for Human Rights

UNHCR— United Nations High Commissioner for Refugees

UNICEF— United Nations Children's Fund (originally UN International Children's Emergency Fund)

UNIFEM— United Nations Development Fund for Women

UPE— universal primary education

USAID— United States Agency for International Development

USIP— United States Institute for Peace

WHO— World Health Organization

Wolesi Jirga— lower house of Loya Jirga

Chapter Notes

Preface

1. Haron Amin, interview with the author, October 25, 2007.
2. Mitra K. Shavarini and Wendy R. Robison, *Women and Education in Iran and Afghanistan: An Annotated Bibliography of Sources in English, 1975–2003* (Lanham, MD: Scarecrow Press, 2005), 1.
3. Ibid.
4. Masooda Jalal, "Afghanistan Is Working Toward Gender Equality," in *Afghanistan: Opposing Viewpoints*, ed. John Woodward (Detroit: Greenhaven Press, 2006), 58. *See also* Jalal, Masooda, "Afghanistan," Remarks at the 49th Session of the UN Commission of the Status of Women, March 2005, www.un.org/webcast/csw2005/statements/050302afghanistan-e.pdf (accessed May 15, 2008).
5. Amin interview, October 25, 2007.
6. Ibid.
7. Ibid.
8. Lina Abirafeh, "An Opportunity Lost? Engaging Men in Gendered Interventions: Voices from Afghanistan," *Journal of Peacebuilding & Development* 3, no. 3 (2007).

Chapter 1

1. World Bank, *Afghanistan: National Reconstruction and Poverty Reduction — the Role of Women in Afghanistan's Future*, xi, http://siteresources.worldbank.org/AFGH ANISTANEXTN/Resources/Afghanistan-GenderReport.pdf (accessed May 15, 2008).
2. Ibid.
3. Rosemarie Skaine, *The Women of Afghanistan Under the Taliban* (Jefferson, NC: McFarland, 2002), 53.
4. Louis Dupree, *Afghanistan* (Princeton, NJ: Princeton University Press, 1980), xx.
5. Rosemarie Skaine, "Soviet-Afghan War (1979–1989)," in *Ground Warfare: An International Encyclopedia*, vol. 3, ed. Stanley L. Sandler, (Santa Barbara, CA: ABC-CLIO, 2002), 828.
6. Skaine, *The Women of Afghanistan*, 8.
7. World Bank, *Afghanistan: Role of Women*, xi.
8. Skaine, *The Women of Afghanistan*, 156–160.
9. Ibid., 8.
10. "Afghanistan's Bonn Agreement One Year Later: A Catalog of Missed Opportunities," *Human Rights News*, December 5, 2002, http://www.hrw.org/backgrounder/asia/afghanistan/bonnlyr-bck.htm (accessed May 15, 2008).
11. "Government-Afghan Bonn Agreement," Afghanistan Government Web Site, afghangovernment.com, http://www.afg hangovernment.com/AfghanAgreement Bonn.htm (accessed May 15, 2008).
12. United States, Congress, House, Committee on Foreign Affairs, *Afghanistan on the Brink: Where Do We Go from Here?* Hearing, February 15, 2007 (Washington: Government Printing Office, 2007), 3,

http://foreignaffairs.house.gov/110/33319. pdf (accessed May 15, 2008); United States, Department of State, Office of the Senior Coordinator for International Women's Issues, "U.S. Commitment to Women in Afghanistan," Fact Sheet, January 3, 2006, http://www.state.gov/g/wi/rls/58651.htm (accessed May 15, 2008).

13. "U.S. Welcomes Afghan President Karzai's Cabinet Appointments: Afghanistan's New Cabinet Favors Technocrats over Warlords," america.gov, December 27, 2004, http://www.america.gov/st/washfile-english/2004/December/200412271409 27ndyblehs0.771847.html (accessed May 15, 2008); United States, Department of State, International Women's Issues, Fact Sheet; Feminist Majority Foundation, "Afghanistan's New Cabinet Includes Three Women," *Feminist Daily News Wire*, January 11, 2005, http://www.feminist.org/news /newsbyte/uswirestory.asp?id=8832 (accessed May 15, 2008).

14. United States, Department of State, International Women's Issues, Fact Sheet.

15. United Nations, IRIN, Office for the Coordination of Humanitarian Affairs, "Afghanistan: Humanitarian Country Profile," January 2007, http://www.irinnews. org/country.aspx?CountryCode=AFG& RegionCode=ASI (accessed May 15, 2008).

16. Ibid.

17. Ibid.

18. "Afghanistan," in *UNICEF Humanitarian Action Report 2008*, 26, http://www. unicef.org/har08/files/HAR_2008_FULL_ Report_English.pdf (accessed May 15, 2008).

19. Ibid.

20. "UNHCR to Resume Afghan Refugees Repatriation from Pakistan from March 1," *China View*, February 28, 2008, http://news.xinhuanet.com/english/2008– 02/28/content_7687420.htm (accessed May 15, 2008).

21. United Nations, IRIN, "Afghanistan: Humanitarian Country Profile."

22. Human Rights Watch, "Afghanistan: Events of 2006," *World Report 2007*, http:// hrw.org/englishwr2k7/docs/2007/01/11/afg han14863.htm (accessed May 15, 2008).

23. Ibid.

24. Ibid.

25. "Inside the Taliban," National Geographic Channel, October 1, 2007.

26. United States, Congress, House, Committee on International Relations, *Afghanistan: Five Years after 9/11*, Hearing, September 20, 2006, Washington: Government Printing Office, 2006, 1.

27. United States, Congress, House, *Afghanistan: Five Years after 9/11*, 2.

28. Henry J. Hyde and Mark Kirk, letter to the president of the United States, September 7, 2006, in United States, Congress, House, *Afghanistan: Five Years after 9/11*, 3.

29. Thom Shanker and Steven Lee Myers, "Afghan Mission Is Reviewed as Concerns Rise," *New York Times*, December 16, 2007, http://www.nytimes.com/ 2007/12/16/washington/16afghan.html?_r= 1&th=&adxnnl=1&oref=slogin&emc=th&a dxnnlx=1197860669-foTgLpZEucL825z6 OqWgAA (accessed May 15, 2008).

30. Ibid.

31. Ibid.

32. Transparency International, "Corruption Perceptions Index 2007," http:// www.transparency.org/policy_research/sur veys_indices/cpi/2007 (accessed May 15, 2008).

33. Transparency International, "Persistent Corruption in Low-income Countries Requires Global Action," press release, September 26, 2007, http://www.transparency. org/news_room/latest_news/press_releases/ 2007/2007_09_26_cpi_2007_en (accessed May 15, 2008).

34. Transparency International, "Corruption Perceptions Index 2005," http:// www.transparency.org/policy_research/sur veys_indices/cpi/2005 (accessed May 15, 2008).

35. Barnett R. Rubin, "Statement," in United States, Congress, House, *Afghanistan: Five Years after 9/11*, 53.

36. Ibid.

37. Haron Amin interview with the author, October 25, 2007.

38. Ibid.

39. Abdul Raheem Yaseer, assistant di-

rector of the Center for Afghanistan Studies, University of Nebraska at Omaha, interview with the author, September 13, 2007.

40. "Afghanistan Study Group Report: 'Revitalizing Our Efforts, Rethinking Our Strategies,'" Center for the Study of the Presidency, http://www.thepresidency.org/pubs/Afghan_Study_Group_highlights.pdf (accessed May 15, 2008).

41. Ibid.

42. Ibid.

43. Amnesty International, "Afghanistan: Taleban Attacks Against Civilians Increasing and Systematic," press release, April 19, 2007, http://web.amnesty.org/library/Index/ENGASA110022007?open&of=ENG-AFG (accessed May 15, 2008).

44. Ibid.

45. Human Rights Watch, "Afghanistan: Events of 2006," *World Report 2007*.

46. Jim Michaels, "Taliban Fighters Escalate Attacks," *USA Today*, November 15, 2007.

47. Ibid.

48. Richard Norton-Taylor, "Afghanistan 'Falling into Taliban Hands,'" *Guardian*, November 21, 2007, http://www.guardian.co.uk:80/afghanistan/story/0,,2214813,00.html (accessed May 15, 2008).

49. Ibid.

50. Karen DeYoung, "U.S. Notes Limited Progress in Afghan War," *Washington Post*, November 25, 2007, http://www.washingtonpost.com/wp-dyn/content/story/2007/11/25/ST2007112500076.html?hpid=moreheadlines (accessed May 15, 2008).

51. ABC Radio Australia, "Afghanistan: Resurgent Taliban Threaten Stability," January 22, 2008, http://www.radioaustralia.net.au/programguide/stories/200801/s2142899.htm (accessed May 15, 2008).

52. VOA News, "Rebel Attacks Kill 12 in Southern Afghanistan," January 21, 2008, http://www.voanews.com:80/english/2008-01-21-voa2.cfm (accessed May 15, 2008).

53. "Afghanistan War Is Just Beginning: Report," *Herald Sun*, January 19, 2008, http://www.news.com.au/heraldsun/story/0,21985,23075709-5005961,00.html (accessed May 15, 2008).

54. Graeme Smith, "Optimism Turns to Gloom in Karzai's Hometown," globeandmail.com, January 25, 2008, http://www.theglobeandmail.com/servlet/story/LAC.20080125.AFGHANKANDAHAR25/TPStory/TPInternational/Asia (accessed May 15, 2008).

55. Ibid.

56. Associated Press, "NATO Says Insurgency Is Not Spreading in Afghanistan," *12 KFVS Heartland News*, February 3, 2008, http://www.kfvs12.com:80/Global/story.asp?S=7815151&nav=8H3x (accessed May 15, 2008).

57. Amin interview, October 25, 2007.

58. Ibid.

59. Ibid.

60. United Nations, Development Fund for Women (UNIFEM), "Women in Afghanistan," *Fact Sheet*, August 2006.

61. United States, Congress, House, *Afghanistan on the Brink*, 3; United States, Department of State, "U.S. Commitment to Women in Afghanistan," Fact Sheet.

62. Yaseer interview, September 13, 2007.

63. Center for Policy and Human Development, Kabul University, *Afghanistan Human Development Report 2007: Bridging Modernity and Tradition: Rule of Law and the Search for Justice* (Islamabad: Army Press, 2007), 3, http://www.undp.org.af/Publications/KeyDocuments/nhdr07_complete.pdf (accessed May 16, 2008).

64. *Afghanistan Now*, January 2007, USAID, http://www.usaid.gov/locations/asia_near_east/documents/countries/afghanistan/afgh_now_0107.pdf (accessed May 16, 2008).

65. Center for Policy and Human Development, *Afghanistan Human Development Report 2007*, 3.

66. Ibid., 19–20.

67. Ibid., 20.

68. Amin, interview, October 25, 2007.

69. M. Ashraf Haidari, "Afghanistan: Beyond Security Issue, the Economy Is Booming," *Eurasianet*, January 24, 2008, http://www.eurasianet.org:80/departments/insight/articles/eav012408b.shtml (accessed May 16, 2008).

70. Human Rights Watch, "Afghanistan: Events of 2006," *World Report 2007*.

71. Center for Policy and Human Development, *Afghanistan Human Development Report 2007*, 4–5.

72. Human Rights Watch, "Afghanistan: Events of 2006," *World Report 2007*.

73. Zoya, RAWA member, "Five Years Later, Afghanistan Still in Flames," transcript of a speech at Afghan Women's Mission benefit for RAWA, "Breaking the Propaganda of Silence," Hollywood, California, October 7, 2006, http://www.rawa.org/zoya_oct7–06.htm (accessed May 16, 2008).

74. Mariam Rawi, RAWA member, "Women in Afghanistan Today: Hopes, Achievements and Challenges," speech, University of South Australia, April 27, 2006, http://www.rawa.org/rawi-speech.htm (accessed May 16, 2008).

75. Amnesty International, "Afghanistan: Women Still under Attack — a Systematic Failure to Protect," AI Index: ASA 11/007/2005, May 30, 2005, http://web.amnesty.org/library/index/engasa11007 2005 (accessed May 16, 2008).

76. Ibid.

77. Neil Genzlinger, "Discovering Pockets of Hope for Afghan Women," *New York Times*, September 15, 2007, http://www.nytimes.com/2007/09/15/arts/television/15genz.html?th&emc=th (accessed May 16, 2008).

78. Sharmeen Obaid-Chinoy, "Afghanistan: Lifting the Veil," Transcript, CNN, September 15, 2007, http://www6.lexisnexis.com/publisher/EndUser?Action= UserDisplayFullDocument&orgId=574& topicId=100007219&docId=1:67030 2846&start=6 (accessed May 16, 2008).

79. Ibid.

80. Amin interview, October 25, 2007.

81. Lina Abirafeh, "An Opportunity Lost? Engaging Men in Gendered Interventions: Voices from Afghanistan," *Journal of Peacebuilding & Development* 3, no. 3 (2007), introduction.

82. Amnesty International, "Afghanistan: Women Still under Attack."

83. Amnesty International, "Afghanistan: All Who Are Not Friends, Are Enemies: Taleban Abuses Against Civilians," AI Index: ASA 11/001/2007, April 19, 2007, http://web.amnesty.org/library/Index/ENGAS A110012007?open&of=ENG-AFG (accessed May 16, 2008).

84. Yaseer interview, September 13, 2007.

85. Ibid.

86. Ibid.

87. Amnesty International, "Afghanistan: All Who Are Not Friends, Are Enemies."

88. Steve Inskeep and Jackie Northam, "Pakistani Military Launches Strikes," NPR, "Morning Edition," January 21, 2008, http://www.npr.org:80/templates/story/story.php?storyId=18279063 (accessed May 16, 2008).

89. Kathy Gannon, "New Taliban Chief Entering Limelight," *USA Today*, January 26, 2008, http://content.usatoday.com/community/utils/idmap/28790387.story (accessed May 16, 2008).

90. Amnesty International, "Afghanistan: All Who Are Not Friends, Are Enemies."

91. Barnett R. Rubin and Abubakar Siddique, "Resolving the Pakistan-Afghanistan Stalemate," United States Institute of Peace, Special Report 176, October 2006, 1–2, http://www.usip.org/pubs/specialreports/sr176.pdf (accessed May 16, 2008).

92. "Inside the Taliban," National Geographic Channel.

93. Amin interview, October 25, 2007.

94. Marvin G. Weinbaum, "Afghanistan and Its Neighbors: An Ever Dangerous Neighborhood," United States Institute of Peace, Special Report 162, June 2006, 1–2, http://www.usip.org/pubs/specialreports/sr162.pdf (accessed May 18, 2008).

95. Amin interview, October 25, 2007.

Chapter 2

1. United Nations Development Fund for Women (UNIFEM), "Gender Profile of the Conflict in Afghanistan," WomenWarPeace.org, http://www.womenwarpeace.org/webfm_send/51 (accessed May 16, 2008).

2. Zahir Tanin interview with the author, New York, November 8, 2007.

3. Ibid.

4. Ibid.

5. Amnesty International, "Afghanistan: All Who Are Not Friends, Are Enemies."

6. Ibid.

7. Nick Meo, "Leaked Aid Map of Afghanistan Reveals Expansion of No-go Zones," *Timesonline*, December 5, 2007, http://www.timesonline.co.uk/tol/news/w orld/asia/article3000067.ece (accessed May 16, 2008).

8. Ann Scott Tyson, "NATO's Not Winning in Afghanistan, Report Says," *Washington Post*, January 31, 2008, A18, http://www.washingtonpost.com/wp-dyn/content/article/2008/01/30/AR200801 3004314.html (accessed May 16, 2008).

9. "Afghanistan," in *UNICEF Humanitarian Action Report 2008*, 26, http://www.unicef.org/har08/files/HAR_2008_FULL_Report_English.pdf (accessed May 15, 2008).

10. Amnesty International, "Afghanistan: All Who Are Not Friends."

11. Ibid.

12. Ibid.

13. Jason Burke, "The New Taliban," *Observer*, October 14, 2007, http://www.guardian.co.uk/afghanistan/story/0,,21908 73,00.html (accessed May 18, 2008).

14. Ibid.

15. Soraya Sarhaddi Nelson, "Taliban's Shifting Tactics Define Afghanistan Conflict," *NPR*, March 4, 2008, http://www.npr.org/templates/story/story.php?sto ryId=87863445 (accessed May 16, 2008).

16. Burke, "The New Taliban."

17. Ibid.

18. Antonio Giustozzi, *Koran, Kalashnikov, and Laptop: The Neo-Taliban Insurgency in Afghanistan* (New York: Columbia University Press, 2008); Sreeram Chaulia, "Book Review: Black Turbans Rebound: *Koran, Kalashnikov and Laptop* by Antonio Giustozzi," *Asia Times Online*, January 26, 2008, http://www.atimes.com/atimes/South_Asia/JA26Df01.html (accessed May 18, 2008).

19. Amnesty International, "Afghanistan: All Who Are Not Friends."

20. Ibid.

21. Ibid.; "A New Layeha [book of rules] for the Mujahedeen," Lucy Powell and Toby Axelrod, translators, from the Swiss weekly, *Die Weltwoche*, November 29, 2006, SignsandSight.com, http://www.signand sight.com/features/1071.html (accessed May 16, 2008).

22. Max L. Gross, *A Muslim Archipelago: Islam and Politics in Southeast Asia* (Washington, DC: National Defense Intelligence College, 2007), 104.

23. Ibid., xiv.

24. Ibid., 242.

25. Ibid., 243.

26. Amnesty International, "Afghanistan: All Who Are Not Friends."

27. Ibid.

28. Ibid.

29. Human Rights Watch, "Afghanistan: Events of 2006," *World Report 2007*.

30. Abdul Raheem Yaseer interview with the author, September 13, 2007.

31. Ibid.

32. Human Rights Watch, "Afghanistan: Events of 2006," *World Report 2007*.

33. Haron Amin interview with the author, October 25, 2007.

34. Ibid.

35. Ibid.

36. Ibid.

37. Ibid.

38. Ibid.

39. Amnesty International, "Afghanistan: All Who Are Not Friends."

40. "Afghan Children in Greatest Peril since 2002: UNICEF," *Canadian Press*, October 25, 2007, http://www.cbc.ca/world/story/2007/10/25/afghan-children.html (accessed May 16, 2008).

41. Associated Press, "Worst Afghan Death Toll Since 2001," *CBSNews.com*, November 7, 2007, http://www.cbsnews.com/stories/2007/11/06/terror/main3457216.shtml?source=RSSattr=HOME_3457216 (accessed May 16, 2008).

42. Associated Press, "Afghan Children Were Deliberately Shot after Suicide Attack, UN Says," *iht.com* (*International Herald Tribune*), November 19, 2007, http://www.iht.com:80/articles/ap/2007/11/19/

asia/AS-GEN-Afghan-Bombing-Aftermath.php (accessed May 16, 2008).

43. Edith M. Lederer, "UN Condemns Violence in Afghanistan," *USA Today*, November 5, 2007, http://www.usatoday.com/news/world/2007-11-05-3963072919_x.htm (accessed May 16, 2008).

44. Associated Press, "Afghanistan Violence Peaks," *MSNBC.com*, October 2, 2007, http://www.msnbc.msn.com/id/2109 2845 (accessed May 16, 2008).

45. David Rohde, "Afghan Suicide Attacks Rising, Report Shows," *NYTimes.com*, September 9, 2007, http://www.nytimes.com/2007/09/09/world/asia/09 afghan.html?n=Top%2fReference%2fTime s%20Topics%2fOrganizations%2fT%2fTa liban%20 (accessed May 16, 2008).

46. Alix Kroeger, "Afghan Civilian Deaths Alarm UN," *BBC News*, November 20, 2007, http://news.bbc.co.uk/2/hi/sou th_asia/7104804.stm (accessed May 16, 2008).

47. Carl Robichaud, "Private Military Contractors also Creating Problems in Afghanistan," *worldpoliticsreview.com*, October 30, 2007, http://www.worldpoliticsre view.com/article.aspx?id=1287 (accessed May 16, 2008).

48. Ibid.

49. Ibid.

50. Lederer, "UN Condemns Violence."

51. Tanin interview, November 8, 2007.

52. Ibid.

53. Anne Cubilié, *Women Witnessing Terror* (New York: Fordham University Press, 2005), 216.

54. Deniz Kandiyoti, "Between the Hammer and the Anvil: Post-Conflict Reconstruction, Islam and Women's Rights," *Third World Quarterly* 28, no. 3 (2007), 503.

55. Tanin interview, November 8, 2007.

56. Amin interview, October 25, 2007.

57. *Afghanistan Now*, January 2007, http://www.usaid.gov/locations/asia_ near_east/documents/countries/afghanista n/afgh_now_0107.pdf (accessed May 16, 2008).

58. Kandiyoti, 503.

59. Amin interview, October 25, 2007.

60. Lina Abirafeh, *Afghanistan Gozargah: Discourses on Gender-Focused Aid in the Aftermath of Conflict*, unpublished Ph.D. dissertation, Development Studies Institute, London School of Economics and Political Science, November 2007, 6.

61. Kandiyoti, 503.

62. Ibid., 506.

63. Ibid.

64. Yaseer interview, September 13, 2007.

65. Ibid.

66. Amin interview, October 25, 2007.

67. Inter-Parliamentary Union, "Women's Suffrage: A World Chronology of the Recognition of Women's Rights to Vote and to Stand for Election," n.d., http://www.ipu.org/wmn-e/suffrage.htm (accessed May 16, 2008).

68. Inter-Parliamentary Union, *Women in Politics: 60 Years in Retrospect* (data valid as at February 1, 2006), "Historical Table," 1, http://www.ipu.org/PDF/publications/wmninfokit06_en.pdf (accessed May 16, 2008).

69. International Institute for Democracy and Electoral Assistance (IDEA) and Stockholm University, "Global Database of Quotas for Women: Afghanistan," May 3, 2006, http://www.quotaproject.org/displayCoun try.cfm?CountryCode=AF (accessed May 16, 2008).

70. United States, Department of State, Office of the Senior Coordinator for International Women's Issues, "U.S. Commitment to Women in Afghanistan," Fact Sheet, January 3, 2006, http://www.state.gov/g/wi/rls/58651.htm (accessed May 16, 2008).

71. Inter-Parliamentary Union, "Women in National Parliaments: World Classification," http://www.ipu.org/wmn-e/classif.htm (accessed May 16, 2008); IPU, "Afghanistan: General Information about the Parliamentary Chamber or Unicameral Parliament," September 18, 2005, http://www.ipu.org/parline-e/reports/2381_A.htm and http://www.ipu.org/parline-e/re ports/2382_A.htm (accessed May 16, 2008); United Nations and IPU, *World Map of Women in Politics 2008*, February

29, 2008, http://www.un.org/av/photo/de
tail/0170711.html (accessed May 16, 2008);
"Women MPS: Afghanistan Ranks 27th,"
Online International News Network,
http://www.onlinenews.com.pk/details.ph
p?id=125159 (accessed May 16, 2008).
72. Kandiyoti, 509–510.
73. Amin interview, October 25, 2007.
74. United Nations, Development Fund
for Women (UNIFEM), "UNIFEM
Afghanistan Fact Sheet 2007," http://www.
unama-afg.org/docs/_UN-Docs/_fact-
sheets/07mayUNIFEM-fact-sheet.pdf (accessed May 16, 2008).
75. Ibid.
76. Nasrine Gross, "Then and Now:
Afghan Women Emerging and Disappearing: The Quest for Women's Rights in
Afghanistan: Comparison of the 1960's
Feminist Movement with Now," Middle
East Studies Association Annual Conference, Boston, November 18–21, 2006.
77. Ibid.
78. Ibid.
79. U.S. Department of State, "Afghan
Women Judges Pursue Legal Training in
United States," June 23, 2006, http://us
info.state.gov/sa/Archive/2006/Jun/
26-824456.html (accessed May 16, 2008).
80. IRIN, UN Office for the Coordination of Humanitarian Affairs, "Afghanistan:
Interview with Head of Independent
Human Rights Body," December 22, 2004,
http://www.irinnews.org/report.a
spx?reportid=26556 (accessed May 16,
2008).
81. Ibid.
82. U.S. Department of State, "United
States Condemns Slaying of Afghan
Women's Rights Advocate," September 26,
2006, http://www.america.gov/st/washfile-
english/2006/September/2006092617073
4mlenuhret0.2518732.html (accessed May
16, 2008).
83. IRIN, "Afghanistan: Interview."
84. Ibid.
85. U.S., Department of State, "Afghan
Women's Struggles, Triumphs Highlighted
in Documentaries," September 26, 2006,
http://www.america.gov/st/washfile-en
glish/2007/June/20070625160452GLnes

noM0.5876734.html (accessed May 16,
2008).
86. U.S., Department of State, "Afghan
Women's Struggles."

Chapter 3

1. Lina Abirafeh, "An Opportunity
Lost? Engaging Men in Gendered Interventions: Voices from Afghanistan," *Journal of
Peacebuilding & Development* 3, no. 3
(2007), introduction.
2. Haron Amin interview with the author, October 25, 2007.
3. Ibid.
4. Ibid.
5. *Afghanistan Now*, January 2007,
http://www.usaid.gov/locations/asia_
near_east/documents/countries/afghanista
n/afgh_now_0107.pdf (accessed May 16,
2008).
6. Ibid., 15.
7. Amin interview, October 25, 2007.
8. Ibid.
9. Ibid.
10. Ibid.
11. *Afghanistan Now*, January 2007, 15.
12. "Drugs Boom, Continued Violence
in Afghanistan for 2008: NATO," AFP,
January 2, 2008, http://afp.google.com/ar
ticle/ALeqM5iLjejGvvpdinmIL2x5g8B7V
nBMGg (accessed May 16, 2008).
13. *Afghanistan Now*, January 2007, 3,
5.
14. IRIN, UN Office for the Coordination of Humanitarian Affairs, "Afghanistan:
UN Prepares for Repatriation of over Half
a Million Refugees," December 5, 2007,
http://www.irinnews.org/report.aspx?Re
portId=75696 (accessed May 16, 2008).
15. IRIN, "Afghanistan: Multiple Humanitarian Challenges in 2008 — Outgoing UN Envoy," December 31, 2007,
http://www.irinnews.org/Report.aspx?Re
portId=76044 (accessed May 16, 2008).
16. Sayed Salahuddin, "Snow Brings
Wonder, Misery for Homeless Afghans,"
Reuters, January 24, 2008, http://www.
reuters.com/article/homepageCrisis/

idUSSP40885._CH_.2400 (accessed May 16, 2008).

17. Deniz Kandiyoti, "Between the Hammer and the Anvil: Post-Conflict Reconstruction, Islam and Women's Rights," *Third World Quarterly* 28, no. 3 (2007), 510.

18. Ibid., 512–513.

19. Nasrine Abou-Bakre Gross, *Women in the Koran: Dari Translation of Verses in the Koran that Mention Women* (Kabul: Roqia Center for Women's Rights, Studies and Education in Afghanistan, 2003).

20. Nasrine Gross, "Then and Now: Afghan Women Emerging and Disappearing: The Quest for Women's Rights in Afghanistan: Comparison of the 1960's Feminist Movement with Now," Middle East Studies Association Annual Conference, Boston, November 18–21, 2006.

21. Abdul Razaq Asmar, *Four-Year Period Main Achievements of MOWA*, Afghanistan, Ministry of Women's Affairs, January 2007, http://www.mowa.gov.af/content/about_mowa/mowa_acheivements_eng.pdf (accessed May 16, 2008); Hassan Banu Ghazanfar, *Performance Report of MoWA For 1384 and 1385 (2005–2006)*, Afghanistan, Ministry of Women's Affairs, March 29, 2007, http://www.mowa.gov.af/content/about_mowa/reports/yearly_reports/mowa_performance_report_05_to_06_eng.pdf (accessed May 16, 2008).

22. *Methods for Solving the Issue of Violence*, Afghanistan, Ministry of Women's Affairs, n.d., 1, http://www.mowa.gov.af/content/about_mowa/violence/methods_for_solving_the_issue_of_violence_eng.pdf (accessed May 16, 2008).

23. Ibid.

24. "Definitions of Non-English Terms Used on our Site," Lahore Ahmadiyya Movement for the Propagation of Islam (Ahmadiyya Anjuman Isha'at-e-Islam, Lahore), n.d., http://aaiil.org/text/gloss/definitions.shtml#p (accessed May 16, 2008).

25. *Methods for Solving the Issue of Violence*, 1.

26. Ibid., 2.

27. Nasrine Gross, "Then and Now."

28. Ibid.

29. Zahir Tanin interview with the author, New York, November 8, 2007.

30. Ibid.

31. Amin interview, October 25, 2007.

32. "Gender in Afghanistan," Afghanistan, Ministry of Women's Affairs, 1–2, http://www.mowa.gov.af/content/about_mowa/gender/gender_in_afghanistan/gender_in_afghanistan_eng.pdf (accessed May 16, 2008).

33. Ibid.

34. Ibid., 4.

35. Ibid., 5.

36. Tanin interview, November 8, 2007.

37. Ibid.

38. Ibid.

39. Ibid.

40. *Methods for Solving the Issue of Violence*, 3–4.

41. Kandiyoti, 513.

42. Americans for UNFPA, "Fueled by Abuse: Self-immolation and Family Violence in Central Asia," n.d., http://www.americansforunfpa.org/NetCommunity/Page.aspx?pid=627&srcid=631 (accessed May 16, 2008).

43. Sharmeen Obaid-Chinoy, "Afghanistan: Lifting the Veil."

44. Ibid.

45. Ibid.

46. Abirafeh, "An Opportunity Lost?" Introduction.

47. Ibid. "A Resurgence of Violence, Violence towards Women: A Backlash."

48. Tanin interview, November 8, 2007.

49. Nasrine Gross, "Then and Now."

50. Ibid.

51. Ibid.

52. Ibid.

53. Amin interview, October 25, 2007.

54. Abdul Raheem Yaseer, interview with the author, September 13, 2007.

Chapter 4

1. Nasrine Abou-Bakre Gross, interview with the author, December 18, 2007.

2. Nasrine Abou-Bakre Gross, "Then and Now: Afghan Women Emerging and

Disappearing: The Quest for Women's Rights in Afghanistan: Comparison of the 1960's Feminist Movement with Now," Middle East Studies Association Annual Conference, Boston, November 18–21, 2006.

3. Ibid.

4. See also Nasrine Abou-Bakre Gross, *Qassarikh-e Malalay* (Memories of the First Girls' High School in Afghanistan) (Falls Church, VA: Kabultec-Amdam, 1998). The book is written in Dari. For more information: Afghan Women and Education, http://users.erols.com/kabultec/firstbk.html (accessed May 17, 2008).

5. Nasrine Abou-Bakre Gross, "Then and Now."

6. Ibid.

7. United States, Department of State, Office of the Senior Coordinator for International Women's Issues, "U.S. Commitment to Women in Afghanistan," Fact Sheet, January 3, 2006, http://www.state.gov/g/wi/rls/58651.htm (accessed May 17, 2008).

8. "Afghanistan," in *UNICEF Humanitarian Action Report 2008*, 26, http://www.unicef.org/har08/files/HAR_2008_FULL_Report_English.pdf (accessed May 15, 2008).

9. *2007 Schools Survey Summary Report*, Afghanistan, Ministry of Education (MoE), January 2008, 17, http://www.moe.gov.af (accessed May 17, 2008).

10. Gross interview, December 18, 2007.

11. Ibid.

12. OxFam International, "Free, Quality Education for Every Afghan Child," Oxfam Briefing Paper 93, November 2006, 1, 21, http://www.campaignforeducation.org/resources/Nov2006/education%20for%20every%20afghan%20child.pdf (accessed May 17, 2008).

13. Gross interview, December 18, 2007.

14. "Afghanistan," in *UNICEF Humanitarian Action Report 2008*, 26,

15. World Bank, *Afghanistan: Role of Women*, xiii.

16. IRIN, UN Office for the Coordination of Humanitarian Affairs, "Afghanistan: Too Many Young Children Dying of Preventable Diseases — UNICEF," January 22, 2008, http://www.irinnews.org:80/Report.

aspx?ReportId=76361 (accessed May 17, 2008).

17. Jason Straziuso, "Bush Ignores Afghan School Violence," *USA Today*, January 29, 2008, http://www.usatoday.com/news/world/2008-01-29-3126253227_x.htm (accessed May 17, 2008).

18. Gross interview, December 18, 2007.

19. Ibid.

20. Ibid.

21. Yaseer interview, September 13, 2007.

22. Jason Straziuso, "Attacks on Afghan Students up Sharply," *USA Today*, January 24, 2008, http://www.usatoday.com/news/world/2008-01-23-296714599_x.htm (accessed May 17, 2008).

23. Ibid.

24. Ibid.

25. Ibid.

26. UNESCO, *Education for All (EFA) Global Monitoring Report*, 6th ed. (Paris, France: UNESCO Publishing, 2007), 21, www.unesco.org/education/GMR/2007/Full_report.pdf (accessed May 17, 2008).

27. Ibid., 92.

28. Ibid., 50, 51.

29. Ibid., 37–38.

30. Ibid., 81.

31. "Rebuilding Afghanistan, Education for All," Better World Campaign, http://www.betterworldcampaign.org/issues/international-security/rebuilding-afganistan.html (accessed August 17, 2008).

32. World Bank, *Afghanistan: Role of Women*, xiii.

33. OxFam International, "Free, Quality Education," 2, 3, 9.

34. Ibid., 3, 9.

35. Ibid., 9.

36. Center for Policy and Human Development, Kabul University, *Afghanistan Human Development Report 2007: Bridging Modernity and Tradition: Rule of Law and the Search for Justice* (Islamabad: Army Press, 2007), 23, http://www.undp.org.af/Publications/KeyDocuments/nhdr07_complete.pdf (accessed May 16, 2008).

37. *2007 Schools Survey Summary Report*, Afghanistan, Ministry of Education (MoE), 12.

38. OxFam International, "Free, Quality Education," 1.

39. oanda.com, FXConverter, Afganistan, August 17, 2008, http://www.oanda.com/convert/classic (accessed August 17, 2008).

40. OxFam International, "Free, Quality Education," 1, 15–16.

41. Ibid., 10.

42. UNESCO, *Education for All Global Monitoring Report*, 75.

43. Ibid., 77.

44. OxFam International, "Free, Quality Education," 10–11.

45. Ibid., 1, 18.

46. Human Rights Watch, "Afghanistan: Events of 2006," *World Report 2007.*

47. "Inside the Taliban," National Geographic Channel, October 1, 2007.

48. Ibid.

49. UNESCO, *Education for All Global Monitoring Report*, 74.

50. IRIN, UN Office for the Coordination of Humanitarian Affairs, "Afghanistan: Some Schools More Vulnerable to Attack than Others?" January 2, 2008, http://www.irinnews.org/Report.aspx?ReportId=76067 (accessed May 17, 2008).

51. Straziuso, "Bush Ignores Afghan School Violence."

52. Amnesty International, "Afghanistan: Taleban Attacks Against Civilians."

53. Obaid-Chinoy, "Afghanistan: Lifting the Veil."

54. World Bank, *Afghanistan: Role of Women,* xiii.

55. OxFam International, "Free, Quality Education," 9–10.

56. Obaid-Chinoy, "Afghanistan: Lifting the Veil."

57. World Bank, *Afghanistan: Role of Women,* xiii.

58. OxFam International, "Free, Quality Education," 11.

59. UNESCO, *Education for All Global Monitoring Report*, 159.

60. Ibid., 165.

61. Ibid., 189, 190.

62. Ibid., *Education for All Global Monitoring Report*, 189.

63. Ibid., *Education for All Global Monitoring Report*, 137.

64. Ibid., *Education for All Global Monitoring Report*, 60.

65. Ibid., *Education for All Global Monitoring Report*, 64.

66. "Rebuilding Afghanistan, Education for All," Better World Campaign.

67. UNESCO, *Education for All Global Monitoring Report*, 65.

68. Yaseer interview, September 13, 2007.

69. Gross, interview, December 18, 2007.

70. Ibid.

71. See also "Literacy Training Transforms Lives of Afghan Couples," U.S. Department of State, http://usinfo.state.gov/scv/Archive/2006/Mar/01–152226.html (accessed May 17, 2008).

72. Gross interview, December 18, 2007.

73. Ibid.

74. Ibid.

75. Ibid.

76. Rosemarie Skaine, "Neither Afghan Nor Islam," *Ethnicities* 2 no. 2 (June 2002), 142.

77. Amin interview, October 25, 2007.

78. Skaine, "Neither Afghan Nor Islam," 142.

79. Ibid.

80. Ibid.

81. Ibid.

82. Gross interview, December 18, 2007.

83. Ibid.

84. Ibid.

85. Ibid.

86. Ibid.

87. IRIN, "Afghanistan: Too Many Young Children Dying."

88. Afghanistan Independent Human Rights Commission (AIHRC), *Economic and Social Rights in Afghanistan II*, August 2007, 2, http://www.aihrc.org.af/Rep_ESRII_Eng_Full_Text_30_Aug_2007.pdf (accessed May 17, 2008).

89. Ibid.

90. Ibid.

91. Ibid.

92. Oxfam, Submission to the House of Commons International Development

Committee Inquiry, "*Development Assistance in Insecure Environments: Afghanistan,*" November 2007, 9–10, http://www.afghanconflictmonitor.org/oxfamuksubmission.pdf (accessed May 17, 2008).

93. "UNIFEM Afghanistan Fact Sheet 2007."

94. World Bank, *Afghanistan: Role of Women,* xiv.

95. Ibid., xiv-xv.

96. Nasrine Abou-Bakre Gross, "Then and Now."

97. Carlotta Gall, "The Women of Kabul are Going Back to Work," *Working Mother* 26, no. 4 (April 2003), 50.

98. BBC News, "Afghan Villagers Answer Your Questions," June 19, 2007, http://news.bbc.co.uk/1/hi/world/south_asia/6763865.stm (accessed May 17, 2008).

99. Ibid.

100. Amin interview, October 25, 2007.

101. U.S. Department of State, "Afghan Women Judges Pursue Legal Training."

102. Help the Afghan Children, http://www.helptheafghanchildren.org/programs_computer_literacy.html (accessed May 17, 2008).

Chapter 5

1. "Physicians for Human Rights Finds High Maternal Mortality Ratio in Herat Province, Afghanistan," press release, September 10, 2002, http://physiciansforhumanrights.org/library/2002-09-10.html (accessed May 17, 2008).

2. Amir Shah, "Afghan Child Deaths Plummet," *Guardian,* November 5, 2007, http://www.guardian.co.uk/afghanistan/story/0,,2205234,00.html (accessed March 17, 2008).

3. Martin Bell, "Child Alert Afghanistan: Martin Bell Reports on Children Caught in War," UNICEF, October 25, 2007, http://www.unicef.org/infobycountry/afghanistan_41372.html (accessed May 17, 2008).

4. "UNICEF: Afghanistan Makes Progress in Reducing Child Mortality,"

China View, January 22, 2008, http://news.xinhuanet.com/english/2008-01/22/content_7474608.htm (accessed May 17, 2008); See also United Nations Children's Fund (UNICEF), *The State of the World's Children 2008,* January 24, 2008, http://www.unicef.org/sowc08/report/report.php (accessed May 17, 2008).

5. "Afghanistan," in *UNICEF Humanitarian Action Report 2008,* 26.

6. Afghanistan Independent Human Rights Commission, *Economic and Social Rights in Afghanistan II.*

7. "UNICEF: Afghanistan Makes Progress"; See also UNICEF, *The State of the World's Children 2008.*

8. IRIN, "Afghanistan: Too Many Young Children Dying."

9. Ibid.

10. World Health Organization (WHO), *Country Cooperation Strategy For WHO and Islamic Republic of Afghanistan 2005 to 2009,* First Draft, August 3, 2005, 28, 34–35, http://www.emro.who.int/afghanistan/Media/PDF/CCS_2005.pdf (accessed May 17, 2008).

11. Afghanistan Independent Human Rights Commission, *Economic and Social Rights in Afghanistan,* Section 13.2, 47.

12. World Health Organization, Eastern Mediterranean Regional Office (EMRO), Division of Health System and Services Development (DHS), Health Policy and Planning Unit, *Health Systems Profile, Country: Afghanistan,* May 14, 2005, 34, 35, http://www.emro.who.int/afghanistan/Media/PDF/HealthSystemProfile-2005.pdf (accessed May 17, 2008).

13. Afghanistan Ministry of Public Health, *Afghanistan Health Sector Balanced Scorecard National and Provincial Results,* Round 3, 2006, i, http://www.jhsph.edu/refugee/response_service/afghanistan/Afghanistan_Balanced_Scorecard.pdf (accessed August 21, 2008).

14. Afghanistan, Ministry of Public Health, Afghanistan Development Forum, Health Sector Presentation, 2007, 2, 3, http://www.adf.gov.af/src/speeches/Health%20Sector%20Presentation.pdf (accessed May 17, 2008).

15. Afghanistan, Ministry of Public Health, "Progress and Challenges of Ministry of Public Health of Afghanistan," February 4, 2008, http://www.moph.gov.af (accessed May 17, 2008).

16. Afghanistan, Ministry of Public Health, Afghanistan Development Forum, 2007, 3.

17. Ibid.

18. Amin interview, October 25, 2007.

19. Bell, "Child Alert Afghanistan."

20. "The World Factbook: Afghanistan," Central Intelligence Agency, https://www.cia.gov/library/publications/the-world-factbook/geos/af.html (accessed May 18, 2008).

21. Afghanistan Independent Human Rights Commission, Economic and Social Rights in Afghanistan II.

22. OxFam, "Free, Quality Education."

23. World Health Organization (WHO), Country Cooperation Strategy, 5.

24. "Afghanistan," in UNICEF Humanitarian Action Report 2008, 26.

25. World Bank, Afghanistan: Role of Women, xii.

26. Shah, "Afghan Child Deaths Plummet."

27. Bell, "Child Alert Afghanistan."

28. World Bank, Afghanistan: Role of Women, xii, xiii.

29. World Health Organization, Country Cooperation Strategy, 14.

30. World Bank, Afghanistan: Role of Women, xii.

31. "UNIFEM Afghanistan Fact Sheet 2007."

32. World Health Organization, Country Cooperation Strategy, 19.

33. "UNIFEM Afghanistan Fact Sheet 2007."

34. UNICEF, "Asia and the Pacific: Afghanistan: Feature Story," Humanitarian Action Report 2008, http://www.unicef.org/har08/index_afghanistan_feature.html (accessed May 17, 2008).

35. World Health Organization, Eastern Mediterranean Regional Office, Health Systems Profile, 6.

36. IRIN, UN Office for the Coordination of Humanitarian Affairs, "Afghanistan:

Losing Hope — Women in Afghanistan," June 18, 2007, http://www.irinnews.org/Report.aspx?ReportId=72775 (accessed May 17, 2008).

37. IRIN, "Afghanistan: Losing Hope."

38. Douglas Huber, "Accelerating Birth Spacing Practices in Afghanistan," ANE Best Practices Conference, Bangkok, Thailand, September 2–8, 2007, 3, http://www.esdproj.org/site/DocServer/CC3_Douglas_Huber_Afghanistan.pdf?docID=948 (accessed May 17, 2008).

39. Ibid., 21.

40. Ibid., 27.

41. Ibid., 28.

42. IRIN, "Afghanistan: Losing Hope."

43. Amin interview, October 25, 2007.

44. IRIN, "Afghanistan: Losing Hope."

45. The World Health Organization, Eastern Mediterranean Regional Office, Health Systems Profile, 6.

46. World Bank, Afghanistan: Role of Women, xii.

47. Afghanistan Now, January 2007, 11.

48. Aryn Baker, "A Decade of De-mining," Time, December 4, 2007, http://www.time.com/time/world/article/0,8599,1690545,00.html (accessed May 17, 2008).

49. C. J. Chivers, "On Taliban Turf, Long Lines of Ailing Children," New York Times, December 12, 2007, http://www.nytimes.com/2007/12/12/world/asia/12afghan.html?ei=5070&en=d0e392e5be2e502e&ex=1198126800&pagewanted=all# (accessed May 17, 2008).

50. Ibid.

51. Kris Torgeson, "After 24 Years of Independent Aid to the Afghan People Doctors Without Borders Withdraws from Afghanistan Following Killings, Threats, and Insecurity," Médecins Sans Frontières Doctors Without Borders, press release, July 28, 2004, http://www.doctorswithoutborders.org/pr/2004/07-28-2004.cfm (accessed May 17, 2008).

52. World Health Organization, Country Cooperation Strategy, 51–53.

53. Ibid., 22.

54. Ibid., 23.

55. Ibid.

56. Barbara Lopes Cardozo et al., Cen-

ters for Disease Control and Prevention, Atlanta, "High Rates of Mental Health Symptoms Reported in Afghanistan," *JAMA* 292 (2004), 575–584; also published on Medical News Today, August 4, 2004, http://www.medicalnewstoday.com/articles/11641.php (accessed August 21, 2008).

57. World Health Organization, *Country Cooperation Strategy*, 48.

58. Ibid., 24.

59. Ibid.

60. Sima Samar, "Human Rights and Women's Rights in Afghanistan," Stephen A. Ogden Jr. Memorial Lecture, Brown University, May 28, 2005, http://www.brown.edu/Administration/News_Bureau/2004–05/04–143.html (accessed May 17, 2008).

61. Amin interview, October 25, 2007.

62. World Health Organization, *Country Cooperation Strategy*, 40.

Chapter 6

1. Lina Abirafeh, research notes, e-mail to Rosemarie Skaine, March 3, 2008.

2. Lina Abirafeh, *Afghanistan Gozargah*, Abstract.

3. Ibid., 176–177.

4. Ibid., 268.

5. Ibid., 269.

6. Ibid., 270.

7. Ibid., 268.

8. Ibid., 273.

9. Ibid., 274.

10. Ibid., 274–275.

11. Ibid., 275.

12. Ibid., 276.

13. Ibid., 278.

14. Ibid., 280–281.

15. Ibid., 282–283.

16. Rosemarie Skaine, "Neither Afghan Nor Islam," *Ethnicities* 2 no. 2 (June 2002), 142.

17. "Habiba Sarabi," *Wikipedia*, http://en.wikipedia.org/wiki/Habiba_Sarabi (accessed May 18, 2008); "Interview with Habiba Sarabi, Governor of Bamiyan," Embassy of Afghanistan, Tokyo, http://www.afghanembassyjp.com/interview6sarabi.html (accessed May 18, 2008).

18. Ibid.

19. Ibid.

20. Ibid.

21. Ibid.

22. "Afghan Women Edging Toward Bigger Roles in Public Life: Interview with Habiba Sarabi, Minister of Culture and Education," ZENIT, September 15, 2002, http://www.zenit.org/article-5344?l=english (accessed May 18, 2008).

23. Allison Lampert, "Beyond Kandahar, an Oasis," *Montreal Gazette*, January 26, 2008, http://www.canada.com/montrealgazette/story.html?id=337d809f-c980–4210-a963–84be57d76888&k=44706 (accessed May 18, 2008).

24. "Interview with Habiba Sarabi."

25. Ibid.

26. "Map of Bamiyan Province," Afgha.com, http://www.afgha.com/?q=node/5170 (accessed May 18, 2008).

27. Paul Anderson, "Afghanistan's First Woman Governor," *BBC News*, June 9, 2005, http://news.bbc.co.uk/1/hi/world/south_asia/4610311.stm (accessed May 18, 2008).

28. "Biography of Dr. Husn Banu Ghazanfar, Minister of MoWA," Afghanistan Ministry of Women's Affairs (MoWA), http://www.mowa.gov.af/content/about_mowa/minister_bio_eng.html (accessed May 18, 2008); "Members of President Hamid Karzai's Cabinet," Afghanistan Online, http://www.afghan-web.com/politics/cabinet_members.html (accessed May 18, 2008).

29. Alisa Tang, "Female Afghan Minister Pushes for Rights," washingtonpost.com, November 22, 2006, http://www.washingtonpost.com/wp-dyn/content/article/2006/11/22/AR2006112200257.html (accessed May 18, 2008).

30. *Methods for Solving the Issue of Violence*, 1.

31. Ibid., 2.

32. *Gender in Afghanistan*, 1–2.

33. Abdul Razaq Asmar, *Four-Year Period Main Achievements of MOWA*, Afghanistan Ministry of Women's Affairs (MoWA),

January 2007, http://www.mowa.gov.af/
content/about_mowa/mowa_acheivemen
ts_eng.pdf (accessed May 18, 2008); Hassan Banu Ghazanfar, *Performance Report Of
MOWA For 1384 and 1385 (2005–2006)*,
Afghanistan Ministry of Women's Affairs
(MoWA), March 29, 2007, http://www.
mowa.gov.af/content/about_mowa/re
ports/yearly_reports/mowa_performance_
report_05_to_06_eng.pdf (accessed May
18, 2008).

34. "Women's Rights Campaigns
Launched in Afghanistan," *Radio Free Eu-
rope/Radio Liberty Newsline* 12 no. 4 (January 7, 2008), http://www.rferl.org/news
line/2008/01/6-swa/swa-070108.asp (accessed May 18, 2008).

35. "Biography of Dr. Husn Banu
Ghazanfar."

36. Tang, "Female Afghan Minister
Pushes for Rights."

37. Ibid.

38. "Her Excellency, Ambassador Zahida Ansary," Embassy of Afghanistan,
Sofia, Bulgaria, http://embassyofafghan
istansofia.org/bio.php (accessed May 18,
2008).

39. "Women and Power In Central Asia
(Part 3): Afghan Women Rise To Top After
Taliban Repression," Radio Free Europe/
Radio Liberty, December 29, 2005, http://
www.rferl.org/featuresarticle/2005/12/7
6696c3d-6774–40f6-ac3f-1c381d8e6583.
html (accessed May 18, 2008).

40. "Her Excellency, Ambassador Zahida Ansary."

41. "Golden Award for Best Diplomatic
Activities Given to H.E. Zahida Ansary,"
February 28, 2008, http://embassyofafghan
istansofia.org/medial.php?news_id=177&st
art=0&category_id=1&parent_id=1&ar
cyear=&arcmonth= (accessed May 18,
2008).

42. Ibid.

43. "Her Excellency, Ambassador Zahida Ansary."

44. Ibid.

45. Zahida Ansary speech, Embassy of
Afghanistan, Sofia, Bulgaria, http://em-
bassyofafghanistansofia.org/maulana.php
(accessed May 18, 2008).

46. Ibid.

47. Zahida Ansary NATO speech, Embassy of Afghanistan, Sofia, Bulgaria,
"NATO Speech," http://embassyofafghan
istansofia.org/nato.php (accessed May 18,
2008).

48. Ibid.

49. Ibid.

50. "Cal Poly Professor Appointed
Afghan Ambassador to Germany," Cal Poly,
News Release, September 5, 2006, http://
calpolynews.calpoly.edu/news_releases/
2006/September/ambassador.html (accessed May 18, 2008).

51. Ibid.

52. "H.E. Maliha Zulfacar — Guest of
KAS," Konrad Adenauer Stiftung Afghanistan Office, October 8, 2006, http://www.
kas.de/proj/home/events/80/2/veranstal
tung_id-22765/index.html (accessed May
18, 2008).

53. "Maliha Zulfacar, Afghanistan's Ambassador to Germany: People in Afghanistan
Need More Tangible Changes," Qantarade,
February 3, 2007, http://www.qantara.de/
webcom/show_article.php/_c-478/_nr-
574/i.html?PHPSESSID= (accessed May
18, 2008).

54. Jennifer Ludden, "Afghan Returns to
Collect the Stories of Her People," NPR,
January 13, 2006, http://www.npr.org/tem
plates/story/story.php?storyId=5151380
(accessed May 18, 2008).

55. "Cal Poly Professor Appointed."

56. "Maliha Zulfacar, Afghanistan's Ambassador to Germany: People in Afghanistan
Need More Tangible Changes."

57. Ibid.

58. Jennifer Ludden, "Afghan Returns to
Collect the Stories"; "Maliha Zulfacar,
Afghanistan's Ambassador to Germany:
People in Afghanistan Need More Tangible
Changes"; "Afghanistan New Ambassadors
to Germany, India and Qatar," Afghanistan
Ministry of Foreign Affairs, September 26,
2006. http://www.mfa.gov.af/detail.asp?
Lang=e&Cat=1&ContID=57 (accessed
May 18, 2008).

59. "PXP Advisor Fatima Gailani Appointed President of Afghan Red Crescent
Society," *Peace Times*, ed. 39, Peace X

Peace, Announcements, February 14, 2005, http://www.peacexpeace.org/resources/newsletters/newsletter39.asp (site discontinued May 18. 2008).

60. Ali Hakimi, "Women and Children Are the First Targets of War," *World Volunteer Web*, March 8, 2007, http://www.worldvolunteerweb.org/browse/countries/afghanistan/doc/women-children-are.html (accessed May 18, 2008).

61. Ibid.; "Interview with Ms Fatima Gailani, President of the Afghan Red Crescent Society," International Committee of the Red Cross, March 31, 2007, http://www.icrc.org/Web/Eng/siteeng0.nsf/html/review-865-p7 (accessed May 18, 2008).

62. Hakimi, "Women and Children Are the First Targets of War."

63. Ibid.

64. "Interview with Ms Fatima Gailani, President of the Afghan Red Crescent Society," *International Review of the Red Cross* 89, no. 865 (March 2007), 9, http://www.icrc.org/Web/eng/siteeng0.nsf/htmlall/review-865-p7/$File/irrc-865-Gailani.pdf (accessed May 2008).

65. "From AUB to Afghanistan," *Main Gate, American University of Beirut Quarterly Magazine* 2, no. 2 (Spring 2004), http://wwwlb.aub.edu.lb/~webmgate/spring04/feature3.html (accessed May 18, 2008); Nasrine Abou-Bakre Gross, interview with the author, December 18, 2007.

66. Gross interview, December 18, 2007.

67. Ibid.

68. Ibid.

69. Ibid.

70. Ibid.

71. Ibid.

72. Ibid.

73. Nasrine Abou-Bakre Gross, *Women's Guide to Winning in the 2005 Afghan Elections*, translated from Dari, United States: SUNY/USAID Afghanistan Parliamentary Assistance Project, July 2005. See also http://www.kabultec.org/womensguide.doc (accessed August 24, 2008).

74. Nasrine Gross, "Profile of the Female Candidates through a Tour of Afghanistan: Report of Workshops for Parliamentary and Provincial Council Elections," Roqia Center for Rights, Studies and Education, November 2005, http://www.kabultec.org/afgtourrpt.html (accessed May 18, 2008).

75. Gross interview, December 18, 2007.

76. Afghan Women, Roqia Center for Rights, Studies and Education, http://www.kabultec.org (accessed May 18, 2008).

77. Gross interview, December 18, 2007.

78. Ibid.

79. "Dr. Sima Samar," Afghanland.com, 2004. http://afghanland.com/history/samar.html (accessed February 26, 2008); "Sima Samar," Profile in Courage Award Recipients, May 24, 2004, http://www.jfklibrary.org/Education+and+Public+Programs/Profile+in+Courage+Award/Award+Recipients/Sima+Samar/ (accessed February 28, 2008).

80. "Biography: Sima Samar," Afghanistan Online, April 12, 2005, http://www.afghan-web.com/bios/today/sima_samar.html (accessed February 27, 2008).

81. "Biography: Sima Samar," Afghanistan Online; "Sima Samar Bibliography," *Wikipedia*, http://en.wikipedia.org/wiki/Sima_Samar (accessed February 23, 2008).

82. "Profile: Sima Samar," BBC, World: South Asia, December 6, 2001, http://news.bbc.co.uk/1/hi/world/south_asia/1695842.stm (accessed February 27, 2008).

83. "Dr. Sima Samar," Afghanland.com, 2004.

84. "The 100 Most Powerful Women: #92 Dr. Sima Samar," Forbes.com, August 30, 2007, http://www.forbes.com/lists/2007/11/biz-07women_Dr-Sima-Samar_C7J2.html (accessed February 27, 2008).

85. "The 100 Most Powerful Women: #92 Dr. Sima Samar," Forbes.com.

86. Sima Samar, "Human Rights and Women's Rights in Afghanistan," Stephen A. Ogden Jr. Memorial Lecture, Brown University, May 28, 2005, http://www.brown.edu/Administration/News_Bureau/2004-05/04-143.html (accessed February 27, 2008).

87. Sima Samar, "Human Rights and Women's Rights."

88. "Sima Samar Bilography," *Wikipedia*.

89. United States, Department of State,

Bureau of International Information Programs, "U.S. Welcomes Afghan President Karzai's Cabinet Appointments: Afghanistan's New Cabinet Favors Technocrats over Warlords," December 27, 2004, http://usinfo.state.gov/xarchives/display.ht ml?p=washfile-english&y=2004&m= December&x=20041227140927ndyblehs 0.771847&t=l ivefeeds/wf-latest.html (accessed September 26, 2007); United States, Department of State, Office of the Senior Coordinator for International Women's Issues, "U.S. Commitment to Women in Afghanistan," Fact Sheet, January 3, 2006, http://www.state.gov/g/wi/rls/58651.htm (accessed September 24, 2007); Feminist Majority Foundation, "Afghanistan's New Cabinet Includes Three Women," *Feminist Daily News Wire*, January 11, 2005, http://www.feminist.org/news/newsbyte/uswirest ory.asp?id=8832 (accessed September 26, 2007).

90. "CNN Live at Daybreak," CNN, Afghan Election, aired October 5, 2004, http://transcripts.cnn.com/TRAN SCRIPTS/0410/05/lad.01.html (accessed February 28, 2008).

91. Nick Meo, "Afghanistan: The Woman Who Wants to Be President," *Afghan Observer*, August 4, 2004, http://afghanob server.com/ResourceCenter/Jalal_0804200 4.html (accessed February 28, 2008).

92. "Massouda Jalal," *Wikipedia*, February 10, 2008, http://en.wikipedia.org/wiki/ Massouda_Jalal (accessed May 27, 2008).

93. Nick Meo, "Afghanistan: The Woman Who Wants to Be"; Kate Clark, "Profile: Massouda Jalal," BBC, June 12, 2002, http://news.bbc.co.uk/1/hi/world/ south_asia/2040523.stm (accessed February 28, 2008).

94. Nick Meo, "Afghanistan: The Woman Who Wants to Be."

95. Nick Meo, "Afghanistan: The Woman Who Wants to Be."

96. Massouda Jalal, "Women's Leadership in Afghanistan's Reconstruction," Asian Social Issues Program, September 8, 2005, http://www.asiasource.org/asip/jalal. cfm (accessed February 28, 2008).

97. Massouda Jalal, "Women's Leadership."

98. Massouda Jalal, "Women's Leadership."

99. "Massouda Jalal," *Wikipedia*.

Chapter 7

1. Tanin interview, November 8, 2007.

2. Hamid Karzai, "Afghanistan Is Becoming Stable," in *Afghanistan: Opposing Viewpoints*, ed. John Woodward (Detroit: Greenhaven Press, 2006), 135.

3. Lina Abirafeh, *Lessons from Gender-focused International Aid in Post-Conflict Afghanistan Learned?* (Bonn, Germany: Friedrich-Ebert-Stiftung Foundation, Division for International Cooperation Department for Development Policy, 2005), 4, http://www.fesgenero.org/media/File/ mulheres_politicas/FES_gender_in_IC_20 05.pdf (accessed May 18, 2008).

4. Karzai, "Afghanistan Is Becoming Stable," 135.

5. Tanin interview, November 8, 2007.

6. Abirafeh, *Lessons from Gender-focused International Aid*, 4.

7. Ibid., 18.

8. Abirafeh, "An Opportunity Lost?" Introduction.

9. "Gender in Afghanistan," 1–2.

10. "Interview with Ms Fatima Gailani," 9.

11. Abirafeh, *Afghanistan Gozargah*, 184, 282–283.

12. Amin interview, October 25, 2007.

13. Ibid.

14. Ibid.

15. Tanin interview, November 8, 2007.

16. Amin interview, October 25, 2007.

Bibliography

ABC Radio Australia. "Afghanistan: Resurgent Taliban Threaten Stability." January 22, 2008. http://www.radio australia.net.au/programguide/stories/200801/s2142899.htm (accessed May 15, 2008).

Abdul Razaq, Asmar. *Four-Year Period Main Achievements of MOWA*. Afghanistan Ministry of Women's Affairs (MoWA). January 2007. http://www.mowa.gov.af/content/about_mowa/mowa_acheivements_eng.pdf (accessed May 18, 2008).

Abirafeh, Lina. *Afghanistan Gozargah: Discourses on Gender-Focused Aid in the Aftermath of Conflict*. Unpublished Ph.D. dissertation, Development Studies Institute, London School of Economics and Political Science, November 2007.

_____. *Lessons from Gender-focused International Aid in Post-Conflict Afghanistan Learned?* Bonn, Germany: Friedrich-Ebert-Stiftung Foundation, Division for International Cooperation Department for Development Policy, 2005. http://www.fesgenero.org/media/File/mulheres_politicas/FES_gender_in_IC_2005.pdf (accessed May 18, 2008).

_____. "An Opportunity Lost? Engaging Men in Gendered Interventions: Voices from Afghanistan." *Journal of Peacebuilding & Development* 3, no. 3 (2007).

"Afghan Children in Greatest Peril since 2002: UNICEF." *Canadian Press*, October 25, 2007. http://www.cbc.ca/world/story/2007/10/25/afghan-children.html (accessed May 16, 2008).

"Afghan Women Edging Toward Bigger Roles in Public Life: Interview with Habiba Sarabi, Minister of Culture and Education." ZENIT, September 15, 2002. http://www.zenit.org/article-5344?l=english (accessed May 18, 2008).

Afghan Women, Roqia Center for Rights, Studies and Education, http://www.kabultec.org (accessed May 18, 2008).

Afghanistan. Ministry of Public Health. Afghanistan Development Forum, Health Sector Presentation, 2007. http://www.adf.gov.af/src/speeches/Health%20Sector%20Presentation.pdf (accessed May 17, 2008).

_____. _____. "Progress and Challenges of Ministry of Public Health of Afghanistan." February 4, 2008. http://www.moph.gov.af (accessed May 17, 2008).

Afghanistan Independent Human Rights Commission (AIHRC), *Economic and Social Rights in Afghanistan II*, August 2007. http://www.aihrc.org.af/Rep_ESRII_Eng_Full_Text_30_Aug_2007.pdf (accessed May 17, 2008).

"Afghanistan New Ambassadors to Germany, India and Qatar." Afghanistan Ministry of Foreign Affairs, September 26, 2006. http://www.mfa.gov.af/detail.asp?Lang=e&Cat=1&ContID=57 (accessed May 18, 2008).

Afghanistan Now. USAID. January 2007. http://www.usaid.gov/locations/asia_near_east/documents/countries/afghanistan/afgh_now_0107.pdf (accessed May 16, 2008).

"Afghanistan Study Group Report: 'Revitalizing Our Efforts, Rethinking Our Strategies.'" Center for the Study of the Presidency, January 30, 2008. http://www.thepresidency.org/pubs/Afghan_Study_Group_highlights.pdf (accessed May 15, 2008).

"Afghanistan War Is Just Beginning: Report." *Herald Sun*, January 19, 2008. http://www.news.com.au/heraldsun/story/0,21985,23075709-5005961,00.html (accessed May 15, 2008).

"Afghanistan's Bonn Agreement One Year Later: A Catalog of Missed Opportunities." *Human Rights News*, December 5, 2002. http://www.hrw.org/backgrounder/asia/afghanistan/bonn1yr-bck.htm (accessed May 15, 2008).

"Afghanistan's New Cabinet Includes Three Women." *Feminist Daily News Wire*, January 11, 2005. http://www.feminist.org/news/newsbyte/uswirestory.asp?id=8832 (accessed May 15, 2008).

Americans for UNFPA. "Fueled by Abuse: Self-immolation and Family Violence in Central Asia," n.d. http://www.americansforunfpa.org/NetCommunity/Page.aspx?pid=627&srcid=631 (accessed May 16, 2008).

Amin, Haron. Interview with the author, October 25, 2007.

Amnesty International. "Afghanistan: Taleban Attacks Against Civilians Increasing and Systematic." Press release, April 19, 2007. http://web.amnesty.org/library/Index/EGASA110022007?open&of=ENG-AFG (accessed May 15, 2008).

_____. "Afghanistan: Women Still under Attack — a Systematic Failure to Protect." AI Index: ASA 11/007/2005, May 30, 2005. http://web.amnesty.org/library/index/engasa110072005 (accessed May 16, 2008).

Anderson, Paul. "Afghanistan's First Woman Governor." *BBC News*, June 9, 2005. http://news.bbc.co.uk/1/hi/world/south_asia/4610311.stm (accessed May 18, 2008).

Ansary, Zahida. Speech, "Culture." Embassy of Afghanistan, Sofia, Bulgaria. http://embassyofafghanistansofia.org/maulana.php (accessed May 18, 2008).

_____. NATO speech. Embassy of Afghanistan, Sofia, Bulgaria, "NATO Speech," 2007. http://embassofafghanistansofia.org/nato.php (accessed May 18, 2008).

Associated Press. "Afghan Children Were Deliberately Shot after Suicide Attack, UN Says." *iht.com* (*International Herald Tribune*), November 19, 2007. http://www.iht.com:80/articles/ap/2007/11/19/asia/AS-GEN-Afghan-Bombing-Aftermath.php (accessed May 16, 2008).

_____. "Afghanistan Violence Peaks." *MSNBC.com*, October 2, 2007. http://www.msnbc.msn.com/id/21092845 (accessed May 16, 2008).

_____. "NATO Says Insurgency Is Not Spreading in Afghanistan." *12 KFVS Heartland News*, February 3, 2008. http://www.kfvs12.com:80/Global/story.asp?S=7815151&nav=8H3x (accessed May 15, 2008).

_____. "Worst Afghan Death Toll Since 2001." *CBSNews.com*, November 7, 2007. http://www.cbsnews.com/stories/2007/11/06/terror/main3457216.shtml?source=RSSattr=HOME_345721 6 (accessed May 16, 2008).

Baker, Aryn. "A Decade of De-mining." *Time*, December 4, 2007. http://www.time.com/time/world/article/0,8599,1690545,00.html (accessed May 17, 2008).

Bell, Martin. "Child Alert Afghanistan: Martin Bell Reports on Children Caught in War." UNICEF, October 25, 2007. http://www.unicef.org/in

fobycountry/afghanistan_41372.html (accessed May 17, 2008).

"Biography of Dr. Husn Banu Ghazanfar, Minister of MoWA." Afghanistan Ministry of Women's Affairs (MoWA), 2006–2008.http://www.mowa.gov.af/content/about_mowa/minister_bio_eng.html (accessed May 18, 2008).

"Biography: Sima Samar." Afghanistan Online, April 12, 2005. http://www.afghan-web.com/bios/today/sima_samar.html (accessed May 18, 2008).

Burke, Jason. "The New Taliban." *Observer*, October 14, 2007. http://www.guardian.co.uk/afghanistan/story/0,,2190873,00.html (accessed May 18, 2008).

"Cal Poly Professor Appointed Afghan Ambassador to Germany." Cal Poly. News Release, September 5, 2006. http://calpolynews.calpoly.edu/news_releases/2006/September/ambassador.html (accessed May 18, 2008).

Cardozo, Barbara Lopes, et al. Centers for Disease Control and Prevention, Atlanta. "High Rates of Mental Health Symptoms Reported in Afghanistan," *JAMA* 292 (2004), 575–584.

Center for Policy and Human Development, Kabul University. *Afghanistan Human Development Report 2007: Bridging Modernity and Tradition: Rule of Law and the Search for Justice* (Islamabad: Army Press, 2007), 3. http://www.undp.org.af/Publications/Key Documents/nhdr07_complete.pdf (accessed May 16, 2008).

Chaulia, Sreeram. "Book Review: Black Turbans Rebound: *Koran, Kalashnikov and Laptop* by Antonio Giustozzi." *Asia Times Online*, January 26, 2008. http://www.atimes.com/atimes/South_Asia/J A26Df01.html (accessed May 18, 2008).

Chivers, C. J. "On Taliban Turf, Long Lines of Ailing Children." *New York Times*, December 12, 2007. http://www.nytimes.com/2007/12/12/world/asia/12afghan.html?ei=5070&en=d0e3

92e5be2e502e&ex=1198126800&page wanted=all# (accessed May 17, 2008).

Clark, Kate. "Profile: Massouda Jalal." BBC News, June 12, 2002. http://news.bbc.co.uk/1/hi/world/south_asia/2040 523.stm (accessed May 18, 2008).

"CNN Live at Daybreak" [Afghan Election]. October 5, 2004. http://tran scripts.cnn.com/TRANSCRIPTS/0410/05/lad.01.html (accessed May 18, 2008).

Cubilié, Anne. *Women Witnessing Terror*. New York: Fordham University Press, 2005.

Davis, Anthony. "How the Taliban Became a Military Force," in *Fundamentalism Reborn? Afghanistan and the Taliban*, ed. William Maley. Washington Square, NY: New York University Press, 1998.

"Definitions of Non-English Terms Used on our Site." Lahore Ahmadiyya Movement for the Propagation of Islam (Ahmadiyya Anjuman Isha'at-e-Islam, Lahore). http://aaiil.org/text/gloss/defini tions.shtml#p (accessed May 16, 2008).

DeYoung, Karen. "U.S. Notes Limited Progress in Afghan War. *Washington Post*, November 25, 2007. http://www.washingtonpost.com/wp-dyn/con tent/story/2007/11/25/ST20071125000 76.html?hpid=moreheadlines (accessed May 15, 2008).

"Dr. Sima Samar." Afghanland.com, 2004. http://afghanland.com/history/samar.html (accessed May 18, 2008).

"Drugs Boom, Continued Violence in Afghanistan for 2008: NATO." AFP, January 2, 2008. http://afp.google.com/article/ALeqM5iLjejGvvpdinm IL2x5g8B7VnBMGg (accessed May 16, 2008).

Forbes.com. "The 100 Most Powerful Women: #28 Dr. Sima Samar." August 31, 2006. http://www.forbes.com /lists/2006/11/06women_Sima-Samar_C7J2.html (accessed May 18, 2008).

_____. "The 100 Most Powerful Women: #92 Dr. Sima Samar." August 30, 2007. http://www.forbes.com/lists/2007/11/biz-07women_Dr-Sima-Samar_C7J2.html (accessed May 18, 2008).

"From AUB to Afghanistan." *Main Gate, American University of Beirut Quarterly Magazine* 2, no. 2 (Spring 2004). http://wwwlb.aub.edu.lb/~webm gate/spring04/feature3.html (accessed May 18, 2008).

Gall, Carlotta. "The Women of Kabul are Going Back to Work," *Working Mother* 26, no. 4 (April 2003).

Gannon, Kathy. "New Taliban Chief Entering Limelight." *USA Today*, January 26, 2008. http://content.usatoday.com/community/utils/idmap/28790387.story (accessed May 16, 2008).

"Gender in Afghanistan." Afghanistan, Ministry of Women's Affairs, 2006–2008. http://www.mowa.gov.af/content/about_mowa/gender/gender_in_afghanistan/gender_in_afghanistan_eng.pdf (accessed May 16, 2008).

Genzlinger, Neil. "Discovering Pockets of Hope for Afghan Women." *New York Times*, September 15, 2007. http://www.nytimes.com/2007/09/15/arts/television/15genz.html?th&emc=th (accessed May 16, 2008).

Ghazanfar, Hassan Banu. *Performance Report of MoWA for 1384 and 1385 (2005–2006)*. Afghanistan Ministry of Women's Affairs (MoWA), March 29, 2007. http://www.mowa.gov.af/content/about_mowa/reports/yearly_reports/mowa_performance_report_05_to_06_eng.pdf (accessed May 18, 2008).

Giustozzi, Antonio. *Koran, Kalashnikov, and Laptop: The Neo-Taliban Insurgency in Afghanistan*. New York: Columbia University Press, 2008.

"Government-Afghan Bonn Agreement." Afghanistan Government Web Site, afghangovernment.com, December 5, 2001. http://www.afghangovernment.com/AfghanAgreementBonn.htm (accessed May 15, 2008).

Gross, Max L. *A Muslim Archipelago: Islam and Politics ins Southeast Asia*. Washington, DC: National Defense Intelligence College, 2007.

Gross, Nasrine Abou-Bakre. Interview with the author, December 18, 2007.

_____. "Profile of the Female Candidates through a Tour of Afghanistan: Report of Workshops for Parliamentary and Provincial Council Elections." Roqia Center for Rights, Studies and Education, November 2005. http://www.kabultec.org/afgtourrpt.html (accessed May 18, 2008).

_____. *Qassarikh-e Malalay* (Memories of the First Girls' High School in Afghanistan). Falls Church, VA: Kabultec-Amdam, 1998.

_____. "Then and Now: Afghan Women Emerging and Disappearing: The Quest for Women's Rights in Afghanistan: Comparison of the 1960's Feminist Movement with Now." Middle East Studies Association Annual Conference, Boston, November 18–21, 2006.

_____. *Women's Guide to Winning in the 2005 Afghan Elections*. Translated from Dari. United States: SUNY/USAID Afghanistan Parliamentary Assistance Project, July 2005.

_____. *Women in the Koran: Dari Translation of Verses in the Koran that Mention Women*. Kabul: Roqia Center for Women's Rights, Studies and Education in Afghanistan, 2003.

"H.E. Maliha Zulfacar — Guest of KAS." Konrad Adenauer Stiftung Afghanistan Office, October 8, 2006. http://www.kas.de/proj/home/events/80/2/veranstaltung_id-22765/index.html (accessed May 18, 2008).

"Habiba Sarabi." Wikipedia, December 2, 2007. http://en.wikipedia.org/wiki/Habiba_Sarabi (accessed May 18, 2008).

Haidari, M. Ashraf. "Afghanistan: Beyond Security Issue, the Economy Is Booming." *Eurasianet,* January 24, 2008. http://www.eurasianet.org:80/departments/insight/articles/eav012408b.shtml (accessed May 16, 2008).

Hakimi, Ali. "Women and Children Are the First Targets of War." *World Volunteer Web,* March 8, 2007. http://www.worldvolunteerweb.org/browse/countries/afghanistan/doc/women-children-are.html (accessed May 18, 2008).

Help the Afghan Children, 2006. http://www.helptheafghanchildren.org/programs_computer_literacy.html (accessed May 17, 2008).

"Her Excellency, Ambassador Zahida Ansary." Embassy of Afghanistan, Sofia, Bulgaria, 2007. http://embassyofafghanistansofia.org/bio.php (accessed May 18, 2008).

Huber, Douglas. "Accelerating Birth Spacing Practices in Afghanistan." ANE Best Practices Conference, Bangkok, Thailand, September 2–8, 2007. http://www.esdproj.org/site/DocServer/CC3_Douglas_Huber_Afghanistan.pdf?docID=948 (accessed May 17, 2008).

Human Rights Watch. "Afghanistan: Events of 2006." *World Report 2007.* http://hrw.org/englishwr2k7/docs/2007/01/11/afghan14863.htm (accessed May 15, 2008).

Hyde, Henry J., and Mark Kirk. Letter to the president of the United States, September 7, 2006, in United States, Congress, House, *Afghanistan: Five Years after 9/11.* Government Printing Office, 2006. http://www.house.gov/international-relations (accessed September 5, 2007).

"Inside the Taliban." National Geographic Channel, October 1, 2007.

Inskeep, Steve, and Jackie Northam. "Pakistani Military Launches Strikes." NPR, "Morning Edition," January 21, 2008. http://www.npr.org:80/templates/story/story.php?storyId=18279063 (accessed May 16, 2008).

International Institute for Democracy and Electoral Assistance (IDEA) and Stockholm University. "Global Database of Quotas for Women: Afghanistan," May 3, 2006. http://www.quotaproject.org/displayCountry.cfm?CountryCode=AF (accessed May 16, 2008).

Inter-Parliamentary Union (IPU). "Afghanistan: General Information about the Parliamentary Chamber or Unicameral Parliament." September 18, 2005. http://www.ipu.org/parline-e/reports/2381_A.htm and http://www.ipu.org/parline-e/reports/2382_A.htm (accessed May 16, 2008).

_____. "Women in National Parliaments: World Classification," February 29, 2008. http://www.ipu.org/wmn-e/classif.htm (accessed May 16, 2008);

_____. *Women in Politics: 60 Years in Retrospect,* February 1, 2006. http://www.ipu.org/PDF/publications/wmninfokit06_en.pdf (accessed May 16, 2008).

_____. "Women's Suffrage: A World Chronology of the Recognition of Women's Rights to Vote and to Stand for Election." http://www.ipu.org/wmn-e/suffrage.htm (accessed May 16, 2008).

"Interview with Habiba Sarabi, Governor of Bamiyan." Embassy of Afghanistan, Tokyo. http://www.afghanembassyjp.com/interview6sarabi.html (accessed May 18, 2008).

"Interview with Ms Fatima Gailani, President of the Afghan Red Crescent Society." International Committee of the Red Cross, March 31, 2007. http://www.icrc.org/Web/Eng/siteeng0.nsf/html/review-865-p7 (accessed May 18, 2008).

"Interview with Ms Fatima Gailani, President of the Afghan Red Crescent Society." *International Review of the Red Cross* 89, no. 865 (March 2007). http://www.icrc.org/Web/eng/siteeng0.nsf/

htmlall/review-865-p7/$File/irrc-865-Gailani.pdf (accessed May 2008).

IRIN, UN Office for the Coordination of Humanitarian Affairs. "Afghanistan: Humanitarian Country Profile. January 2007. http://www.irinnews.org/country.aspx?CountryCode=AFG&RegionCode=ASI (accessed May 15, 2008).

_____. "Afghanistan: Interview with Head of Independent Human Rights Body." December 22, 2004. http://www.irinnews.org/report.aspx?reportid=26556 (accessed May 16, 2008).

_____. "Afghanistan: Losing Hope — Women in Afghanistan. June 18, 2007. http://www.irinnews.org/Report.aspx?ReportId=72775 (accessed May 17, 2008).

_____. "Afghanistan: Multiple Humanitarian Challenges in 2008 — Outgoing UN Envoy." December 31, 2007. http://www.irinnews.org/Report.aspx?ReportId=76044 (accessed May 16, 2008).

_____. "Afghanistan: Some Schools More Vulnerable to Attack than Others?" January 2, 2008. http://www.irinnews.org/Report.aspx?ReportId=76067 (accessed May 17, 2008).

_____. "Afghanistan: Too Many Young Children Dying of Preventable Diseases — UNICEF." January 22, 2008. http://www.irinnews.org:80/Report.aspx?ReportId=76361 (accessed May 17, 2008).

_____. "Afghanistan: UN Prepares for Repatriation of over Half a Million Refugees," December 5, 2007. http://www.irinnews.org/report.aspx?ReportId=75696 (accessed May 16, 2008); Jalal, Masooda. "Afghanistan." Remarks at the 49th Session of the UN Commission of the Status of Women, March 2005. www.un.org/webcast/csw2005/statements/050302afghanistan-e.pdf (accessed May 15, 2008).

Jalal, Massoda. "Afghanistan Is Working Toward Gender Equality." In *Afghanistan: Opposing Viewpoints,* ed. John Woodward. Detroit: Greenhaven Press, 2006.

Jalal, Massouda. "Women's Leadership in Afghanistan's Reconstruction." Asia Source, September 8, 2005. http://www.asiasource.org/asip/jalal.cfm (accessed May 18, 2008).

Kandiyoti, Deniz. "Between the Hammer and the Anvil: Post-Conflict Reconstruction, Islam and Women's Rights." *Third World Quarterly* 28, no. 3 (2007), 503–517.

Karzai, Hamid. "Afghanistan Is Becoming Stable." In *Afghanistan: Opposing Viewpoints,* ed. John Woodward. Detroit: Greenhaven Press, 2006.

Kroeger, Alix. "Afghan Civilian Deaths Alarm UN." *BBC News,* November 20, 2007. http://news.bbc.co.uk/2/hi/south_asia/7104804.stm (accessed May 16, 2008).

Lampert, Allison. "Beyond Kandahar, an Oasis." *Montreal Gazette,* January 26, 2008. http://www.canada.com/montrealgazette/story.html?id=337d809f-c980-4210-a963-84be57d76888&k=44706 (accessed May 18, 2008).

Lederer, Edith M. "UN Condemns Violence in Afghanistan." *USA Today,* November 5, 2007. http://www.usatoday.com/news/world/2007-11-05-396307 2919_x.htm (accessed May 16, 2008).

"Literacy Training Transforms Lives of Afghan Couples." U.S. Department of State, March 1, 2006. http://usinfo.state.gov/scv/Archive/2006/Mar/01-1 52226.html (accessed May 17, 2008).

Ludden, Jennifer. "Afghan Returns to Collect the Stories of Her People." NPR, January 13, 2006. http://www.npr.org/templates/story/story.php?storyId=5151380 (accessed May 18, 2008).

Maley, William. "Introduction: Interpreting the Taliban." In Rosemarie Skaine, *The Women of Afghanistan under the Taliban.* Jefferson, NC: McFarland, 2002.

"Maliha Zulfacar, Afghanistan's Ambassador to Germany: People in Afghanistan Need More Tangible Changes." Qantarade, February 3, 2007. http://www.qantara.de/webcom/show_article.php/_c-478/_nr-574/i.html?PHPSESSID= (accessed May 18, 2008).

"Map of Bamiyan Province." Afgha.com, January 12, 2007. http://www.afgha.com/?q=node/5170 (accessed May 18, 2008).

"Massouda Jalal." *Wikipedia*, February 10, 2008. http://en.wikipedia.org/wiki/Massouda_Jalal (accessed May 18, 2008).

"Members of President Hamid Karzai's Cabinet." Afghanistan Online, September 25, 2007. http://www.afghan-web.com/politics/cabinet_members.html (accessed May 18, 2008).

Meo, Nick. "Afghanistan: The Woman Who Wants to Be President." *Afghan Observer*, August 4, 2004. http://afghanobserver.com/ResourceCenter/Jalal_08042004.html (accessed May 18, 2008).

_____. "Leaked Aid Map of Afghanistan Reveals Expansion of No-go Zones." *Timesonline*, December 5, 2007. http://www.timesonline.co.uk/tol/news/world/asia/article3000067.ece (accessed May 16, 2008).

Methods for Solving the Issue of Violence. Afghanistan, Ministry of Women's Affairs. http://www.mowa.gov.af/content/about_mowa/violence/methods_for_solving_the_issue_of_violence_eng.pdf (accessed May 16, 2008).

Michaels, Jim. "Taliban Fighters Escalate Attacks." *USA Today*, November 15, 2007.

NATO. "Reconstruction and Development (R&D)," November 15, 2007. http://www.nato.int/ISAF/topics/recon_dev/index.html (accessed May 18, 2008).

Nelson, Soraya Sarhaddi. "Taliban's Shifting Tactics Define Afghanistan Conflict." *NPR*, March 4, 2008. http://www.npr.org/templates/story/story.php?storyId=87863445 (accessed May 16, 2008).

"A New Layeha [book of rules] for the Mujahedeen." Lucy Powell and Toby Axelrod, translators, from the Swiss weekly, *Die Weltwoche*, November 29, 2006. SignsandSight.com. http://www.signandsight.com/features/1071.html (accessed May 16, 2008).

Norton-Taylor, Richard. "Afghanistan 'Falling into Taliban Hands.'" *Guardian*, November 21, 2007. http://www.guardian.co.uk:80/afghanistan/story/0,,2214813,00.html (accessed May 15, 2008).

Obaid-Chinoy, Sharmeen. "Afghanistan: Lifting the Veil." Transcript. CNN, September 15, 2007. http://www6.lexisnexis.com/publisher/EndUser?Action=UserDisplayFullDocument&orgId=574&topicId=100007219&docId=1:670302846&start=6 (accessed May 16, 2008).

Oxfam International. "*Development Assistance in Insecure Environments: Afghanistan*" Overview of Priorities. Submission to the House of Commons International Development Committee Inquiry, November 2007. http://www.afghanconflictmonitor.org/oxfamuksubmission.pdf (accessed May 17, 2008).

_____. "Free, Quality Education for Every Afghan Child." Oxfam Briefing Paper 93, November 2006. http://www.campaignforeducation.org/resources/Nov2006/education%20for%20every%20afghan%20child.pdf (accessed May 17, 2008).

PXP Advisor Fatima Gailani Appointed President of Afghan Red Crescent Society." *Peace Times*, ed. 39, Peace X Peace, February 14, 2005. http://www.peacexpeace.org/resources/newsletters/newsletter39.asp (site discontinued May 18, 2008).

"Physicians for Human Rights Finds

High Maternal Mortality Ratio in Herat Province, Afghanistan." Press release, September 10, 2002. http://physicians forhumanrights.org/library/2002–09–10.html (accessed May 17, 2008).

"Profile: Sima Samar." BBC News, December 6, 2001. http://news.bbc.co.uk/1/hi/world/south_asia/1695842.stm (accessed May 18, 2008).

Rawi, Mariam. "Women in Afghanistan Today: Hopes, Achievements and Challenges. Speech, University of South Australia, April 27, 2006. http://www.rawa.org/rawi-speech.htm (accessed May 16, 2008).

"Rebuilding Afghanistan, Education for All." Better World Campaign. http://www.betterworldcampaign.org/issues/international-security/rebuilding-afghanistan.html (accessed August 17, 2008).

Robichaud, Carl. "Private Military Contractors also Creating Problems in Afghanistan." *worldpoliticsreview.com*, October 30, 2007. http://www.worldpoliticsreview.com/article.aspx?id=1287 (accessed May 16, 2008).

Rohde, David. "Afghan Suicide Attacks Rising, Report Shows." *NYTimes.com*, September 9, 2007. http://www.nytimes.com/2007/09/09/world/asia/09afghan.html?n=Top%2fReference%2fTimes%20Topics%2fOrganizations%2fT%2fTaliban%20 (accessed May 16, 2008).

Roqia Center Report for 2007.

Rubin, Barnett R. "Capitol Hill Hearing Testimony." "Testimony, October 8, 1998, Barnett R. Rubin, Director of the Center for Preventive Action and Senior Fellow Senate Foreign Relations near Eastern and South Asian Affairs Events in Afghanistan." *Federal Document Clearing House.*

_____. "Statement." In United States. Congress. House. *Afghanistan: Five Years After 9/11.* Hearing, September 20, 2006. Washington: Government Printing Office, 2006. http://www.house.gov/international-relations (accessed September 5, 2007).

_____, and Abubakar Siddique. "Resolving the Pakistan-Afghanistan Stalemate." United States Institute of Peace, Special Report 176, October 2006. http://www.usip.org/pubs/specialreports/sr176.pdf (accessed May 16, 2008).

Salahuddin, Sayed. "Snow Brings Wonder, Misery for Homeless Afghans." *Reuters*, January 24, 2008. http://www.reuters.com/article/homepageCrisis/idUSSP40885._CH_.2400 (accessed May 16, 2008).

Samar, Sima. "Human Rights and Women's Rights in Afghanistan." Stephen A. Ogden Jr. Memorial Lecture, Brown University, May 28, 2005. http://www.brown.edu/Administration/News_Bureau/2004–05/04–143.html (accessed May 17, 2008).

Shah, Amir. "Afghan Child Deaths Plummet." *Guardian*, November 5, 2007. http://www.guardian.co.uk/afghanistan/story/0,,2205234,00.html (accessed March 17, 2008).

Shanker, Thom, and Steven Lee Myers. "Afghan Mission Is Reviewed as Concerns Rise," *New York Times*, December 16, 2007. http://www.nytimes.com/2007/12/16/washington/16afghan.html?_r=1&th=&adxnnl=1&oref=slogin&emc=th&adxnnlx=1197860669-foTgLpZEucL825z6OqWgAA (accessed May 15, 2008).

Shavarini, Mitra K., and Wendy R. Robison. *Women and Education in Iran and Afghanistan: An Annotated Bibliography of Sources in English 1975–2003.* Lanham, MD: Scarecrow Press, 2005.

"Sima Samar." [Profile in Courage Award winner biography]. John F. Kennedy Library Foundation, May 24, 2004. http://www.jfklibrary.org/Education+and+Public+Programs/Profile+in+Courage+Award/Award+Recipi ents/Sima+Samar (accessed May 18, 2008).

"Sima Samar." *Wikipedia*, February 23, 2008. http://en.wikipedia.org/wiki/Sima_Samar (accessed May 18, 2008).

Skaine, Rosemarie. "Neither Afghan Nor Islam." *Ethnicities* 2 no. 2 (June 2002).

_____. "Soviet-Afghan War (1979–1989)." In *Ground Warfare: An International Encyclopedia*, vol. 3, Stanley L. Sandler, ed. Santa Barbara, Calif.: ABC-CLIO, 2002.

_____. *The Women of Afghanistan Under the Taliban*. Jefferson, NC: McFarland, 2002.

Smith, Graeme. "Optimism Turns to Gloom in Karzai's Hometown." Globeandmail.com, January 25, 2008. http://www.theglobeandmail.com/servlet/story/LAC.20080125.AFGHANKANDAHAR25/TPStory/TPInternational/Asia (accessed May 15, 2008).

Straziuso, Jason. "Attacks on Afghan Students up Sharply." *USA Today*, January 24, 2008. http://www.usatoday.com/news/world/2008-01-23-296714599_x.htm (accessed May 17, 2008).

_____. "Bush Ignores Afghan School Violence." *USA Today*, January 29, 2008. http://www.usatoday.com/news/world/2008-01-29-3126253227_x.htm (accessed May 17, 2008).

Tang, Alisa. "Female Afghan Minister Pushes for Rights." Washingtonpost.com, November 22, 2006. http://www.washingtonpost.com/wp-dyn/content/article/2006/11/22/AR2006112200257.html (accessed May 18, 2008).

Tanin, Zahir. Interview with the author, November 8, 2007.

Torgeson, Kris. "After 24 Years of Independent Aid to the Afghan People Doctors Without Borders Withdraws from Afghanistan Following Killings, Threats, and Insecurity." Médecins Sans Frontières Doctors Without Borders. Press release, July 28, 2004. http://www.doctorswithoutborders.org/pr/2004/07-28-2004.cfm (accessed May 17, 2008).

Transparency International. "Corruption Perceptions Index 2005." http://www.transparency.org/policy_research/surveys_indices/cpi/2005 (accessed May 15, 2008).

_____. "Corruption Perceptions Index 2007." http://www.transparency.org/policy_research/surveys_indices/cpi/2007 (accessed May 15, 2008).

_____. "Persistent Corruption in Low-income Countries Requires Global Action." Press release, September 26, 2007. http://www.transparency.org/news_room/latest_news/press_releases/2007/2007_09_26_cpi_2007_en (accessed May 15, 2008).

2007 Schools Survey Summary Report. Afghanistan, Ministry of Education (MoE). January 2008, 17. http://www.moe.gov.af (accessed May 17, 2008).

Tyson, Ann Scott. "NATO's Not Winning in Afghanistan, Report Says." *Washington Post*, January 31, 2008. http://www.washingtonpost.com/wp-dyn/content/article/2008/01/30/AR2008013004314.html (accessed May 16, 2008).

"U.S. Welcomes Afghan President Karzai's Cabinet Appointments: Afghanistan's New Cabinet Favors Technocrats over Warlords." America.gov, December 27, 2004. http://www.america.gov/st/washfile-english/2004/December/20041227140927ndyblehs0.771847.html (accessed May 15, 2008).

UNESCO. *Education for All (EFA) Global Monitoring Report*, 6th ed. Paris, France: UNESCO Publishing, 2007. www.unesco.org/education/GMR/2007/Full_report.pdf (accessed May 17, 2008).

"UNHCR to Resume Afghan Refugees Repatriation from Pakistan from March 1." *China View*, February 28, 2008. http://news.xinhuanet.com/english/2008-02/28/content_7687420.htm (accessed May 15, 2008).

"UNICEF: Afghanistan Makes Progress in Reducing Child Mortality." *China View*, January 22, 2008. http://news.xinhuanet.com/english/2008–01/22/content_7474608.htm (accessed May 17, 2008).

UNICEF. "Afghanistan: Statistics, Women, 1990–2005." http://www.unicef.org/infobycountry/afghanistan_statistics.html (accessed May 18, 2008).

_____. "Asia and the Pacific: Afghanistan: Feature Story." *Humanitarian Action Report 2008*. http://www.unicef.org/har08/index_afghanistan_feature.html (accessed May 17, 2008).

_____. *Humanitarian Action Report 2008*. http://www.unicef.org/har08/files/HAR_2008_FULL_Report_English.pdf (accessed May 15, 2008).

_____. *The State of the World's Children 2008*. http://www.unicef.org/sowc08/report/report.php (accessed May 17, 2008).

United Nations. Development Fund for Women (UNIFEM). "UNIFEM Afghanistan Fact Sheet 2007." http://www.unama-afg.org/docs/_UN-Docs/_fact-sheets/07mayUNIFEM-factsheet.pdf (accessed May 16, 2008).

_____. "Gender Profile of the Conflict in Afghanistan." WomenWarPeace.org. http://www.womenwarpeace.org/webfm_send/51 (accessed May 16, 2008).

United Nations and IPU. *World Map of Women in Politics 2008*. February 29, 2008. http://www.un.org/av/photo/detail/0170711.html (accessed May 16, 2008).

United States. Congress. House of Representatives. Committee on Foreign Affairs. *Afghanistan on the Brink: Where Do We Go from Here?* Hearing, February 15, 2007. Washington: Government Printing Office, 2007. http://foreignaffairs.house.gov/110/33319.pdf (accessed May 15, 2008).

_____. _____. _____. Committee on International Relations. *Afghanistan: Five Years After 9/11*. Hearing, September 20, 2006. Washington: Government Printing Office, 2006.

_____. Department of State, "Afghan Women Judges Pursue Legal Training in United States." June 23, 2006. http://usinfo.state.gov/sa/Archive/2006/Jun/26–824456.html (accessed May 16, 2008).

_____. _____. "Afghan Women's Struggles, Triumphs Highlighted in Documentaries." September 26, 2006. http://www.america.gov/st/washfile-english/2007/June/20070625160452GLnesnoM0.5876734.html (accessed May 16, 2008).

_____. _____. "United States Condemns Slaying of Afghan Women's Rights Advocate." September 26, 2006. http://www.america.gov/st/washfile-english/2006/September/20060926170734mlenuhret0.2518732.html (accessed May 16, 2008).

_____. _____. Embassy, Kabul, Afghanistan. Economic Section, Fall 2004. http://kabul.usembassy.gov/business_afg.html (page discontinued May 17, 2008).

_____. _____. Office of the Senior Coordinator for International Women's Issues. "U.S. Commitment to Women in Afghanistan." Fact Sheet, January 3, 2006. http://www.state.gov/g/wi/rls/58651.htm (accessed May 15, 2008).

VOA News. "Rebel Attacks Kill 12 in Southern Afghanistan." January 21, 2008. http://www.voanews.com:80/english/2008–01–21-voa2.cfm (accessed May 15, 2008).

Weinbaum, Marvin G. "Afghanistan and Its Neighbors: An Ever Dangerous Neighborhood," United States Institute of Peace. Special Report 162, June 2006. http://www.usip.org/pubs/specialreports/sr162.pdf (accessed May 18, 2008).

"Women and Power in Central Asia (Part

3): Afghan Women Rise to Top After Taliban Repression." Radio Free Europe/Radio Liberty, Dec. 29, 2005. http://www.rferl.org/featuresarticle/2005/12/76696c3d-6774-40f6-ac3f-1c381d8e6583.html (accessed May 18, 2008).

"Women's Rights Campaigns Launched in Afghanistan." *Radio Free Europe/Radio Liberty Newsline* 12 no. 4 (January 7, 2008). http://www.rferl.org/newsline/2008/01/6-swa/swa-070108.asp (accessed May 18, 2008).

World Bank. *Afghanistan: National Reconstruction and Poverty Reduction — The Role of Women in Afghanistan's Future.* http://siteresources.worldbank.org/AFGHANISTANEXTN/Resources/AfghanistanGenderReport.pdf (accessed May 15, 2008).

"The World Factbook: Afghanistan." Central Intelligence Agency. https://www.cia.gov/library/publications/the-world-factbook/geos/af.html (accessed May 18, 2008).

World Health Organization. *Country Co-operation Strategy for WHO and Islamic Republic of Afghanistan 2005 to 2009.* First Draft, August 3, 2005. http://www.emro.who.int/afghanistan/Media/PDF/CCS_2005.pdf (accessed May 17, 2008).

World Health Organization. Eastern Mediterranean Regional Office (EMRO). Division of Health System and Services Development (DHS), Health Policy and Planning Unit. *Health Systems Profile, Country: Afghanistan.* May 14, 2005. http://www.emro.who.int/afghanistan/Media/PDF/HealthSystemProfile-2005.pdf (accessed May 17, 2008).

Yaseer, Abdul Raheem. Interview with the author, September 13, 2007.

Zoya, RAWA member. "Five Years Later, Afghanistan Still in Flames." Transcript of a speech at Afghan Women's Mission benefit for RAWA. "Breaking the Propaganda of Silence," Hollywood, California, October 7, 2006. http://www.rawa.org/zoya_oct7-06.htm (accessed May 16, 2008).

Index

Index